John Hayes is a voice crying out in the wilderness of Western Christian affluence. *Sub-merge* is a chronicle of his conviction that Jesus calls us to attach ourselves uncomfortably to desperate people. His life is a testament to the fact that he really believes what he says. Many can point the finger, but few use their hands to do something about it. Hayes has captured both the prophetic word and the prophetic act in this work. Will we have the courage to not just read a good book but also to live out the truths it contains?

Scott Bessenecker
Director, InterVarsity Global Projects

Whether you are a casual, committed or calloused Christian, this book will enliven your faith, expand your vision and bring you closer to God's broken heart for our troubled world. A wise man once said, "Broken knuckles are like broken hearts; the more they break, the bigger they get." Too many of us in the Church are afraid to break our knuckles or get our hands dirty with the pain of this world. *Sub-merge* gives compelling evidence why this is not only required of the Christian but also is the way of life our Savior calls us live.

John Green
Executive Director, Emmaus Ministries

Of all the books in all the world that will be published this year, John Hayes's deeply uncomfortable heart cry is one of the very few that will, I believe, make the Lord Jesus smile in recognition. Hayes's insights and undoubted authority erupt from a life lived in the seminary of the street and in the sanctuary of the poor. Here we have the theology of praxis recounted passionately and yet with unusual grace. *Sub-merge* is an important book that will equip and encourage us to integrate prayer, mission and mercy in truly biblical worship.

Pete Greig
Cofounder, 24-7 Prayer
Author, *God on Mute, The Vision* and *Red Moon Rising*

Sub-merge is a very significant book, and whilst the particular model of incarnational ministry in the book has been articulated and tested in the white heat contexts of missions to the poorest of the poor, the missional implications of this book extend well beyond the scope of urban mission, to that of missions in general and missions to the West in particular. The fact that this book is written by a courageous, highly articulate, genuinely apostolic practitioner only makes it more appealing and convincing. A must-read for those searching for sustainable ways to meaningfully reach across cultural barriers wherever they might be.

Alan Hirsch
Author, *The Forgotten Ways: Reactivating the Missional Church*

This powerfully prophetic book holds a mirror up to the face of the Western church and forces us to see ourselves against the backdrop of a broken, suffering world. Through jagged-edged human drama and graphic factual data, *sub-merge* offers a penetrating analysis of contemporary global urban reality and provides hopeful strategies for new paradigms of Kingdom work.

Robert Lupton
President, FCS Urban Ministries

John Hayes powerfully communicates the impact that global realities have had on him. Through vivid stories and jarring statistics, Hayes shows how the poverty of affluence has overtaken the materialistic West so that two-thirds of the world's population is invisible to us. *Sub-merge* compels me to stop floating and to dive deep into bringing the love of Christ to the least of these.

Scottie May
Professor, Wheaton College

Finally, we have a book that gives a voice to the cry of the disenfranchised and to the desire deep within our hearts to respond and live an authentic poured-out life. John Hayes writes and lives with the same passion. He lives with the poor and writes for the poor. The Christian order he founded practices what they preach.

Jon Sharpe
Professor, Global Urban Studies, Bakke Graduate University

John Hayes will take you on a trip you will never forget—from San Francisco to Calcutta and Caracas. You will travel in the company of the contemporary Franciscans of InnerCHANGE. They are ordinary people who have taken the call to follow Christ very seriously, devoting their lives to work with some of our poorest neighbors. You will travel to neighborhoods never visited by the tour buses. You will meet the kind of people Jesus hung out with and cared for. Most of all, *submerge* will challenge you to the core to consider following Christ in ways that will change your life.

Tom Sine
Mustard Seed Associates (www.msainfo.org)

God is stirring in the ruins of the "real world," saying again as to St. Francis, "Rebuild my church." John Hayes, backed by a choir of InnerCHANGE storytellers, tells of a new missional order celebrating God's good news in the abandoned places of the world. Those of us who care about the future of the Church need to hear what they've been learning there . . . and join the party.

Jonathan Wilson-Hartgrove
Cofounder, Rutba House
Director, School for Conversion

john b. hayes

sub-merge

Regal

From Gospel Light
Ventura, California, U.S.A.

PUBLISHED BY REGAL BOOKS
FROM GOSPEL LIGHT
VENTURA, CALIFORNIA, U.S.A.
PRINTED IN THE U.S.A.

Regal Books is a ministry of Gospel Light, a Christian publisher dedicated to serving the local church. We believe God's vision for Gospel Light is to provide church leaders with biblical, user-friendly materials that will help them evangelize, disciple and minister to children, youth and families.

It is our prayer that this Regal book will help you discover biblical truth for your own life and help you meet the needs of others. May God richly bless you.

For a free catalog of resources from Regal Books/Gospel Light, please call your Christian supplier or contact us at 1-800-4-GOSPEL or www.regalbooks.com.

Library of Congress Cataloging-in-Publication Data
Hayes, John B. (John Baldwin), 1954-
   Sub-merge / John B. Hayes.
     p. cm.
   1. Christianity and culture. 2. Poverty—Religious aspects—Christianity. 3. Church work with the poor. I. Title.
   BR115.C8H42 2006
   261.8'325—dc22   2006027767

1   2   3   4   5   6   7   8   9   10   /   10   09   08   07   06

Rights for publishing this book in other languages are contracted by Gospel Light Worldwide, the international nonprofit ministry of Gospel Light. Gospel Light Worldwide also provides publishing and technical assistance to international publishers dedicated to producing Sunday School and Vacation Bible School curricula and books in the languages of the world. For additional information, visit www.gospellightworldwide.org; write to Gospel Light Worldwide, P.O. Box 3875, Ventura, CA 93006; or send an e-mail to info@gospellightworldwide.org.

To the man begging in India,

who turned my world upside down

so that I could stand upright;

and to Deanna,

whose love and example help me

maintain that footing.

contents

erge

ING DEEP IN A SHALLOW WORLD

Foreword

When I first met John Hayes in about 1981, I viewed him as a reflection of a young man who seeks to know and do the will of God. At that time, John was employed with an organization called STEP, of which I participated in the original development. Through the years, I have followed John's progress as he developed his own organization, InnerCHANGE, a Christian order composed of communities of missionaries living and ministering incarnationally among the poor.

InnerCHANGE has filled a unique and strategic place in the cause of cross-cultural redemption. John and his colleagues have planted stakes in places few others have dared to go. Often, I have crossed paths with him and his team members. And I was particularly pleased when John recruited a young lady named Tammy Fong Heilemann, who had spent a summer working with us at the John M. Perkins Foundation. You will read some of Tammy's story in this book.

More recently, I shared a taxi in Washington, D.C., with InnerCHANGE's Nate Bacon. We both were en route to participate in a nonviolent protest making our voices heard on behalf of the poor and marginalized. It was the last time in my life I would be arrested (I promised my wife), and it was Nate's first (the gang members in San Francisco now think he is cool). In a way, it was another expression of baton passing to the next generation that will no doubt find new, bold ways to have their voices heard in nonviolent but effective ways.

Over the years, I have been amazed by the quality of people John Hayes has recruited. I have watched as they really submerged themselves into the lives of the people with whom they worked. This has been a real inspiration to me. To honor me by asking me to write the foreword for this book is a real privilege and a blessing.

One of my foundational principles has been what I call the three *Rs* of Christian community development: Relocation, Reconciliation and Redistribution. Relocation means going to the people and living among them. It is best summed up in this Chinese poem:

Go to the people
Live among them
Learn from them
Love them
Start with what they know
Build on what they have
But of the best leaders
When their work is finished
Their task is done
The people will remark
We have done it ourselves.

John has lived out this poem. He has met with the best developers in the world, such as Ray Bakke, Robert Lupton and Tom Sine. He has been inspired by Mother Teresa and others and applied their principles. Through God's grace, John has raised up a team of people and planted them in major cities around the world to affirm the dignity of the people.

When I read this book, the passage that came to me was Romans 10:14-15, where Paul explains Gentile redemption—

cross-cultural redemption—and talks about "How shall they hear without a preacher? And how shall they preach, except they be sent" (*KJV*). Paul then adds, "How beautiful are the feet of them that . . . bring glad tidings of good things!"

Sub-merge tells the story of incarnational ministry. As I see it, incarnational ministry is ultimate reconciliation. It's going into every culture, living among the people, affirming their dignity and loving them. It is carrying the gospel to one village and loving the people so that they can then bring the gospel to the next village and love the people there. When you actually live with the people, that village, that tribal or ethnic group that might be at odds with others will see so clearly and receive this message of God's reconciliation because it's so affirming.

This book needs to be read by the whole church, particularly by anyone who wants to launch mission in the world especially as it relates to cross-culture ministry. We all need to think in these terms, because cross-cultural is where the war is and that's where the violence comes from. The incarnational aspect of the gospel brings the love of God to people. In his gospel, the apostle John writes, "And the word was made flesh and dwelled among us and we beheld his glory, the glory of the only begotten of the father, full of grace and truth."

I believe this book will go a long way in enlightening our society to do mission, especially as we think of the cities of our nation and how they are so multi-racial. We must go into these cultures that have been divided by war, poverty, and race.

This book is a handbook for anyone serious about ministry. It needs to be read by the whole church. The stories told illustrate the power of this incarnational message and the power of this love that burns through racial and cultural barriers. Read it, be as blessed as I was and then go forth with love.

John M. Perkins
Director, John M. Perkins Foundation for
Reconciliation and Development

Introduction

Sub-merge is a manifesto, a prophetic call to join what God is doing among poor and marginalized communities, those who are shut out from or cannot find footing in the market-driven economies of the world. Our planet is spiritually, socially and environmentally at risk, and the vulnerable poor are the first to pay the price. How we respond to this situation, individually and collectively, matters deeply. *Sub-merge* is also a message of hope to Christians around the world, especially First World Christians who yearn to respond to the poor personally but don't know how or are fearful they will be burned out in the process.

In InnerCHANGE, we believe that one response needed today is to create unique orders—*mission communities that are part team, part tribe, part family.* We have journeyed to a place beneath the consumer mirage of status, style, spending and speed. We have experienced change from *sub-merging,* what we call going beneath the surface of a consumer society's demands and aspirations and finding life with Christ among the poor. On this journey, we have learned ways to live deep in this shallow world. *Sub-merge* is written to share some of our insights in this adventure and to outline what we believe are imperatives for other emerging orders in this new world.

Living deep is something that only God can lead us to—it is a direction, not an accomplishment. Living deep concentrates on the welfare of God's people and the pursuit of His Word. By "shallow world" I refer to the "world, the flesh, and the devil," to quote Martin Luther's summary of the forces that assail us and take us in a direction counter to the Kingdom (see 1 John 2:16). I believe the anesthesia of First World affluence enhances the shallow world's pull and makes living deep that much more challenging.

Finally, I wrote *sub-merge* because society and culture are changing so rapidly that many of the Church's traditional responses are being called into question—in particular among the poor. Lessons from forgotten Christian history need to be unearthed. The ground has moved beneath the Church's feet, and for the most part, our attention has been elsewhere while it happened. *Sub-merge* is an effort to see that the terrain we stand on is new ground, new opportunity. This new ground requires deeper responses, deeper spirituality and a deeper sense of community.

Deeper Responses

The new ground will be urban. A large percentage of Christians now realize that seeking the spiritual, social and environmental welfare of cities is more significant to our collective future together than ever before. "Seek the welfare of the city where I have sent you," wrote the prophet Jeremiah, "and pray to the Lord on its behalf for in its peace you will find your own" (Jer. 29:7).

The importance of cities transcends demographics. Cities exert disproportionate influence in shaping twenty-first-century culture. As author and teacher Ray Bakke observes, cities operate as magnets that draw in the world's people and as magnifiers that "breathe out" urban culture everywhere as the desirable norm. Yet mission entities struggle to find appropriate urban strategies. This struggle is particularly apparent for First World missionaries who are unprepared for and unaccustomed to the pressing level of urban poverty. Nearly 1 billion people in the world, one-third of urban residents, live in slums. Even more alarming, slum populations are growing faster than any other demographic sector.[1] More than ever, seeking the welfare of cities means being prepared to seek the welfare of the poor.

The new ground does not have a church building and its ministries at its center. In the developed and developing worlds, the unreached poor dwell in places that are increasingly inaccessible to traditional Christian outreach efforts. For more than two decades, churches in U.S. cities have attempted to use traditional outreach strategies on what is increasingly sophisticated mission ground. But this phenomenon is not limited to the United States. Cities in all parts of the world are socially more complex and diverse than ever before. To succeed and connect among the urban poor, Christian workers will need to acquire new skills in language, culture and community organizing—in fact, they will have to think like apostolic workers, willing to go out to (Greek: *apolluso*) rather than simply draw in the lost and poor.

Beyond the need to communicate with greater skill and relevance to an increasingly post-Christendom world, there is a need for more mission workers who will follow Christ's model and go out *incarnationally.* In using the word "incarnational," we refer to mission that envisions becoming like the people we are praying to reach. The apostle Paul described it well when he said that he attempted to be a Jew to the Jews, weak to the weak, and all things to all men. In an over-messaged world, we must embrace the reality that Kingdom Good News is more likely to be authentically received from among a multitude of voices when people who can be seen, heard and touched communicate it in living form.

Deeper Spirituality

As I spend time with young people in the U.S. and other parts of the West, I find a generation of Christian disciples with an increasingly postmodern outlook and set of expectations. This younger generation seems to be increasingly disenchanted with a faith life that peaks on Sundays and wrestles the remainder of the week in a spiritual crawl space. As I have listened to young disciples, I sense that they do not want to attend church services that confuse worship and entertainment, joy and *enjoy*.

As we have sub-merged among the poor, we have embraced a spirituality centering on an upside-down-kingdom Jesus. Christ reminds us that the last are truly first, the leader is servant, the poor are blessed, and the rich go away empty-handed. Through the years, I have observed that Christian missionaries who have emerged from the mainstream church have often inadvertently communicated that Christianity is a middle-class, Western phenomenon. Consequently, conversion in the field sometimes appears more cultural than spiritual. In Jesus, however, God stands with the poor and the outcast as He promised to do in Matthew 25, and He is available to be met among them in a vital and personal way. We have only just begun to glimpse a spirituality we do not deserve and cannot earn but desperately want more of. This meeting with God's Son among the poor is personal without being exclusive, freeing without being individualistic, and full of a grace that allows us to celebrate who we truly are, not just who we hope to be.

I believe that God is calling for a new kind of missionary with a more holistic understanding of mission and self. Too often, mission-sending entities communicate that mission is primarily a profession. On the other hand, too often churches give the impression that mission is a short-term adventure or rite of passage for the young. As I have heard Fuller Theological Seminary professor Dr. Bobby Clinton state, effective ministry flows out of our being, not just our doing. We must equip our young Christian workers with the conviction that mission is both a vocation and a way of living that is redemptive in our fullest selves.

Deeper Sense of Community

"New wine," Jesus said, "needs to be put in fresh wineskins" (Luke 5:38). Old wineskins, stiff with use, burst when new wine is poured into them. The loss is double, as Jesus points out, because the wine is spilled and the skins are ruined. New wineskins, new mission vehicles, are necessary to mature and preserve the fresh expressions required to help the maturation process of emerging communities and the gifts God has given them.

Although two-thirds of the world's human beings live in poverty or hover close to it, only a small fraction of Christian workers actually go to live and work among them. Piecing statistics together, only about 6 percent of mission workers actually minister as poor to the poor, and that figure may be generous. We have a math problem. Either God is not calling many to do this, or we are not hearing Him. If the good news were a marketable product like Coca-Cola® or Pepsi®, a 6 percent reach to two-thirds of the world would mean that someone in marketing would be fired. Not so in Christendom. Nevertheless, God is well able to work with the many or the few.

Still, as I encounter mission workers among the poor worldwide, the quality of people and their level of commitment excite me. Likewise, I am encouraged by the emergence of new incarnational mission entities targeting the poor and marginalized. Servants to Asia's Poor, a pioneer among Protestant agencies among the poor in the 1970s, has been followed by Urban Neighbors of Hope (UNOH), Word Made Flesh, Servant Partners, Emmaus, and others. In the U.K., there is a host of new creative entities, Urban Expression being the one I know best. In the developing world, too, there are fresh expressions of church planting and mission among the poor, some entirely comprised of nationals, such as Lifeway Mission, based in Nairobi.

Mission man-hours are declining ever more rapidly. Some of this has to do with money. Despite strong sustained economic growth worldwide during the 1990s, mission giving declined. Nowhere is this disparity more apparent than in the U.S. In a land of plenty, missions are on a starvation diet. However, the fall-off in missions is about more than changes in giving patterns; it is also about changing attitudes.

Identifying and helping current and future apostolic communities mature and develop is crucial. To sustain mission workers in challenging ministry among the poor long-term, we must move from training to developing, or forming, individuals. To form individuals and help them gain a sense of their unique destinies, we must first *see* them. At InnerCHANGE, we have discovered that communities, with their effort toward transparent relationships, "see" more accurately than organizational hierarchies do. Orders, which have their emphasis on collective life, can be ideal places to both sharpen and sustain individuals.

Seeking an Other World

Sub-merge addresses four areas of urgency in missions today:

1. Not enough Christian mission workers and volunteers are going out to live and work among the poor.[2]
2. When they do go, they are not staying long enough to make a lasting impact.
3. Mission organizations are not organizing wisely enough to sustain missionaries and truly empower the poor.
4. More Christian men and women with professional backgrounds and/or training need to be creatively drawn in to mission work among the poor so that holistic transformation becomes more attainable in poor communities.

At InnerCHANGE, we are aware of how young we all are in the journey among the poor as communities of mission workers. Although God has done much in and through us that is dear to us, we are painfully aware that our work will appear small in the world's eyes. This book is a manifesto less because of what we have done than of what we have seen. In sub-merging among the poor, we have found that the world looks different from the way it does on the surface. We have seen God in a different way. We have seen Him redefine success and adjust the way we see beauty. *Sub-merge* also represents a manifesto because it is part of a larger body of very articulate voices writing on behalf of the poor. *Sub-merge* joins with and stands on the shoulders of many vital prophets and missionaries whom God has raised for work among the poor.

My prayer as you begin this book is that you will capture something of what it means to live deep lives in a world of tragic and overwhelming human need while being simultaneously pressed by culture to lead shallow lives. Speaking for all of us who work among the poor, we hope that this book contributes to your journey of faith with Christ who sub-merged for us and expresses Himself so vividly below the surface of a shallow world.

Stories

Sub-merge compiles many stories (including sidebars by the InnerCHANGE staff and some of our friends) about our experiences among the poor, as well as stories of kindred spirits.

In writing this book in first person, I would be remiss if I were to imply that my stories among the poor are InnerCHANGE's most compelling. In many ways, they are representative of the middle of the pack. I have found, however, that as a member of a community uniformly pursuing Jesus, middle of the pack, or indeed any other position, is a good and meaningful place to be.

subsistence

\Sub*sist"ence\, n. [Cf. F. subsistence, L subsistentia.] 1. Real being; existence.

substance

\Sub"stance\, v.t. To furnish or endow with substance;
to supply property to; to make rich. [Obs].

substitute

\Sub"stit"ute\, v.t. To put in the place of another person or thing; to exchange.

subdivide

\sub'di*vide"\, v.t. To divide the parts of (anything) into more parts; to part into smaller divisions; to divide again, as what has already been divided.

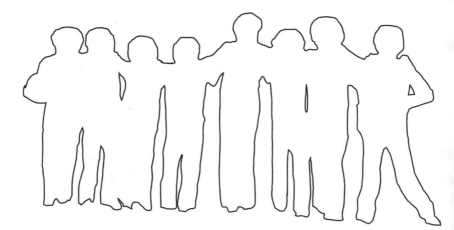

s u b v e r t

\Sub*vert\ v.i. To overthrow anything from the foundation; to be subversive.

submission

\Sub*mis"sion\, n. The act of submitting; the act of yielding to power or authority; surrender of the person and power to the control of government of another; obedience; compliance.

sub-merge

\Sub*merge"\, v.i. [L. submergere, submersum; sub under + mergere to plunge]
To plunge into water or other fluid; to be merged; hence, to be completely included

After this, there is no turning back. You take the blue pill, the story ends. You wake up in your bed and believe whatever you want to believe. You take the red pill, you stay in wonderland, and I show you how deep the rabbit hole goes.

Morpheus (Laurence Fishburne) to Neo (Keanu Reeves) in <u>The Matrix</u>

Caps sail through the air. The crowd's roar crescendos while camera shutters click and lights flash. Parents tuck programs into purses and pockets as keepsakes and rush to the front of the auditorium in search of their graduating loved ones, or they climb up on chairs and wave.

For the graduates, this pomp and circumstance is the last hurrah of youthful exuberance, so they make the most of it. Tomorrow they will have to begin the determined integration into the workforce as adults. No more sleeping until noon and missing class. No more late-night conversations between soul mates about hopes and dreams. No more debates about the world's problems and how this generation can solve them.

For those young people in the United States and other Western countries who do not graduate, or for whom graduation is not a significant event, other rites of passage shepherd them toward the work world. Some take over family businesses; others learn trades as apprentices; a few make it in Hollywood or the sports world. Whether by process or event, the dominant culture sends a clear message: It is time to grow up, shed youthful ideals and make a buck.

Welcome to the real world.

The problem is, most of the
real world doesn't look like this.

In fact, much of the world
looks more like this.

Westerners who journey beyond the borders of wealthy countries to the slums and neighborhoods of the two-thirds world, or to inner cities anywhere, see the contrast. A few ask questions and dare to wonder whether their vision of a reasonable, mainstream, Madison Avenue-driven Western life is actually privileged, even sheltered.

Red pill, blue pill. Which vision of the real world will we choose as we stake out our ground in following Jesus?

In the cult film *The Matrix*, Thomas A. Anderson (played by Keanu Reeves) is an Everyman computer programmer who commutes to the same cubicle daily to write programs for a respectable software company. At night, he furtively freelances at his own terminal as a hacker. When his instincts compel him to go down the rabbit hole, he encounters Morpheus (played by Laurence Fishburne). In an instant, his generic world unravels as he glimpses the sinister reality beneath the veneer. Face to face with Thomas, Morpheus extends a pill in either hand. If Thomas chooses the blue pill, he can dismiss his glimpse of reality's dark side and forget it, as though it were a bad dream. If he takes the red pill, he chooses to experience the world the way it really is, including all its dangers and discomforts. "Remember," Morpheus tells him, "all I am offering is the truth." Thomas takes the red pill, and Morpheus becomes his guide as Thomas enters the grinding reality below the surface world. In the process, Thomas is transformed and fittingly takes his hacker name of Neo to acknowledge his new, deeper identity.

As with the *Matrix*, the surface of Western consumer society conceals a darker, more desperate reality beneath the barrage of carefully crafted images that vie incessantly for our attention. Every year roughly $250 billion is spent on advertising, while half the world—nearly 3 billion people—live on less than $2 a day. Of that number, the World Bank records that 1.3 billion live on less than $1 a day.[3] It is common knowledge now that the gap between the richest and poorest countries continues to steadily widen. As impoverished nations are left behind, their resentment intensifies.[4] What is not as commonly known is the increasing "knowledge gap"—97 percent of patents are owned by industrialized countries, and 80 percent of those held in developing countries belong to foreign nationals from industrialized nations.[5]

However, the magnitude of the problem is more than economic, more than material. As I travel through the world, I see more and more evidence that old-fashioned political colonialism has simply given way to subtle forms of cultural imperialism. First World media today enjoy a nearly limitless reach, even into remote pockets of the world that were inaccessible a decade ago. That, coupled with aggressive marketing by large corporations from the most developed countries, has helped to subdue traditional values like simplicity and modesty and has introduced instead a grab-and-gratify culture obsessed with style and ostentatious display.

Meanwhile, poverty stubbornly persists in some of the wealthiest countries in the world. In the United States, it is estimated that one child in four is born below the official poverty line. A recent U. S. Census reported that despite overall economic growth, the number of poor increased by 1.3 million people in one year.[6] For many Americans, this news comes as no surprise. It is simply a reminder of the ever-present reality that the richest nation in the world, self-described as the land of equal opportunity, is more opportunity than equal.

Red pill, blue pill.

It is refreshing to find that a large proportion of young people in the U.S. and other parts of the West express genuine concern for the plight of the poor. I have also seen that young people who determine to discover ways to act as good Samaritans run into all kinds of obstacles. Parents often prove an impediment to those who would pursue mission among the poor. The Western world's baby-boom generation is now comfortably in command of more resources than any other generation has ever had. Having said that, the most valuable Kingdom resource over which boomers exercise influence is not their bank accounts but their children. Ironically, as idealistic boomers have become parents, they have often resorted to the same phrases their parents used to steer their children. Aside from constant references to the "real world," boomer parents remind their twenty-something children, "You need to get a real job," or "Idealism is great, but what will you live on? Saving the world doesn't pay the bills."

The process by which we let go of our hopes to make a difference for God and settle for making a living is subtle and gradual. In our late teens and early twenties, we promise ourselves we'll defy the rat race, but like lint to a hairball, we get snagged. First we get sidetracked from mission as we pay off school debt. Next we postpone our ideals to squeeze in a little fun time before we get serious. Then we opt for good money (no one ever works for bad money) to prepare for a marriage partner and family. Before we realize it, two decades have passed, and our best intentions to serve the Lord in mission have funneled down the drain of midlife, leaving a bathtub ring of unmet expectations. Or worse, we don't even notice the change that has slowly eclipsed our original dreams as we grow accustomed to a life of second thoughts. What is left is a house, or houses, full of good things, and a vague suspicion that, in the words of poet William Stafford, "we have followed the wrong god home."

Blue pill.

Perhaps it seems that I am unfairly subjecting the Western mainstream's lifestyle and culture to a great deal of criticism, particularly the corporate world's notion of the real world. My intention is to call attention to the fact that to a great degree the corporate world has shaped our worldview considerably and influences the way we look at mission and church. It also influences our critical life choices.

I have been a businessman in both the United States and Japan, two countries shaped enormously by their corporations, and I can attest to the fact that the default setting for a young person choosing vocation is the professional world: business, law or medicine. In addition, the professional marketplace possesses a vocabulary that has become pervasive in our culture and exerts great gravitational pull on life choices. Phrases like "the real world," "bottom line," "successful" and "work ethic" tend to set standards and overshadow the validity of other choices, traditional missions included.

As Christians, we must examine our culture as best we can through the lens of the kingdom of God. The fact that our prominent Christian universities allocate increasing amounts of time to equipping Christians for mission in the marketplace is, to me, a hopeful reaffirmation of mission in a broad sense. It is very helpful to affirm the marketplace as an important calling for young Christians. On the other hand, preparing Christians for the business world now overshadows, and in many quarters has even displaced, formation for traditional mission, especially mission among the poor—I find this not so helpful. During the past three years, I was one of only a handful of speakers on several campuses to address mission among the poor. In my visits to prominent Christian universities, faculty members have expressed concern that their campuses graduate increasingly fewer men and women into full-time mission, here or abroad.

I have journeyed both as a businessman and as a mission worker among the poor. I can look back on both career paths and see God at work. I can also look back and see the shadow that "real world" expectations cast on my life, acting as an undertow on my footing as a Christian. God used a dramatic incident to reshape my perspective.

Red pill.

jagged edges

I have found the paradox, that if you love until it hurts,
there can be no more hurt, only more love.

MOTHER TERESA

Calcutta, April 1980

I stood in line to board a night plane from Tokyo, Japan, to Calcutta, India. I was looking forward to this adventure in India and Nepal that I had been planning for months. I didn't know it at the time, but I was standing at the edge of the rest of my life. In Tokyo, I was a freelance consultant to four large Japanese firms. I was four years out of college as a history major at Princeton. Two of those years I spent as an insurance underwriter in Manhattan, and the other two on my own in Japan.

I was full of confidence and ready for something different. I especially wanted to walk the streets of Calcutta (now Kolkata)—

in those days one of the poorest cities of the world. I wanted to backpack my way, traveling third class so that I could get maximum exposure to India.

I was looking forward to this solo expedition with God. I wanted to test my faith and experience Him in a country so poor, so Hindu and Muslim. It felt like a trip we were planning together, as if He had just checked out of the office one day and said, "I'll go with you." A year and a half earlier, on my twenty-fourth birthday, in the small hours of the night and in the grip of a hangover, I recommitted my life to Christ; and for the first time in my life with God, I had kept my promise to follow Him daily without roller-coasting, submitting every area of my life to Him as best I could. Japan wasn't the most glamorous time of my walk with Him, but it was steady and sure, and in looking back, it was a time of foundational growth.

Someone said, "If you want to make God laugh, tell Him your plans." I thought that God and I had agreed on the kind of enriching, fine-tuning spiritual expedition that would best add depth to my character. I can't say that I expected to become another Mother Teresa; I didn't even know about her in those days. I'm not sure what I expected; I know that I didn't expect God to strip me to the core to get me ready for a new worldview.

That first night, I arrived bleary-eyed at 2:00 A.M. in Calcutta's International airport, a surreal experience of officials herding numb passengers toward lines that formed and re-formed with little outcome in a building that looked like strung-together flypaper. I've read that Calcutta has leapt forward the past two decades, buoyed by a service and technology economy and boasting an elaborate new subway; but in 1980, it was devastatingly poor, with an estimated one-third of its seven million people living as squatters or hand to mouth on the street. There were none of the standard oases for U.S. travelers we've come to expect today even in out-of-the-way places —McDonald's, Pizza Hut, Starbucks—pieces of familiar real estate we can dash into for a few minutes and regain some cultural balance.

For about four days I simply walked pavement, keeping my pockets full of change to give to the beggars that lined the curbs. I had tried hanging on to the overcrowded buses that swayed down the streets but gave it up after a while as too claustrophobic. By early afternoon, the temperature soared to nearly 120 degrees, and by late afternoon, searing winds drove in off the plains and evaporated every drop of moisture on my skin, leaving dried salt rivulets on my arms and rings around my eyes and mouth. In those blistering hours everybody would retreat indoors, leaving the streets to the beggars and the desperate. It became a time when I could actually walk around without pushing and jostling my way. Beggars would call out, "Sahib, Sahib," and follow me into the turf of the next beggars. Often there would be an ugly squabble that so disoriented me, I wondered if I was doing any good, if I had any business being there. Once, I felt a gentle pressure as a man with a deformed arm twisted like a pretzel laid it on my shoulder. I remember flinching and feeling terribly ashamed. I saw whole families on the street, with blind children whose eyes were poked out (one of the terrible effects of poverty in India in those days was that parents were rumored to maim their children at birth to better elicit the sympathy of passersby).

At night I returned to a cellblock of a room. A naked bulb hung from the ceiling. The walls were splattered with tiny blood spots where travelers had smacked mosquitoes, and the lumpy bed creaked like an unsprung trap. I tried to sleep in the bed the first night but soon moved to the floor, wrapping myself in a homemade blanket I'd bought on the street. I tried to journal some reflections, but already my short sojourn alone in India was wearing out the lining of my spiritual depth.

One morning I stepped out of the $3-a-night hotel where I was staying and watched a mother bathe her baby in curb water so thick with waste and oil that I could see the rainbow slick on the surface. Water, any water, is nearly sacred in India. I reminded myself that I had come to India seeking the image of God in people's faces and His hand at work in the activity of the streets. But I had to confess I saw little evidence of Him.

On the fifth day, about midday, I was walking on a major boulevard and came to a corner and noticed a crowd. To notice a crowd in India is like observing a drop of water in the ocean, but in this case, the crowd set itself apart by shouting as if the people were at a sporting event. I was sweaty and tired, but still I was curious. Just before I walked to the edge of the crowd, I remember sensing something faintly ominous. But I was a 25-year-old American, fit from rowing crew in college, and so I thought I'd just go take a look.

In India, independence notwithstanding, a white man was still a *sahib* in those days. When I approached the crowd, they parted respectfully for me so I could walk to the edge of the action.

I was not prepared for what I saw.

Two policemen in khaki uniforms stood over a man who had lost both of his legs from the waist, and a piece of one arm. The officers beat the man with their batons, forcing him to recoil on the ground. All he could do to get away from the police was roll. The crowd parted in a corridor to make space for him to roll. To this day, I have no idea why the crowd was in such frenzy. It was impossible for me to discover whose side they were on or why the police would beat so defenseless a man. Perhaps they were making an object lesson out of him, because begging was purportedly against the law.

As a former college athlete schooled to think first with his body and then with his mind, I was tempted to jump in physically. With rising self-righteousness, I squared off with the two policemen, thinking, *I can waste you two guys.* For a moment the two men stopped, batons in midair, looking uneasy and vaguely embarrassed. Clearly, this Westerner wasn't supposed to see this India.

The policeman closest to me smiled strangely, as if to say, "You're an American; this is our country. If you touch us, we will put you away in a miserable jail for life." I can only imagine what would have happened to me in India had I assaulted those policemen.

After that, my memory is hazy. I think the beggar, who had paused in uncertainty, and perhaps shame, started rolling again. His last glance at me seemed to express pity. The police stepped past me, resumed beating the man, and the crowd closed around me, crying out again in an emotional pitch I could not recognize. Somehow I wandered back to my hotel room and threw myself on the bed and cried. It was as if the image I had so carefully crafted of my life, the identity assembled brick by brick, all the awards and successes, the trophy experiences I had crowded to the front, shattered in that moment of need.

After Calcutta

As I look back, it seems odd that this transforming encounter of my life should last only a few seconds and involve no exchange of words. I had not had an appropriate answer for the horror I faced back on the street, and I felt shame for failing to act.

I continued my trip through India and up into some of the most beautiful terrain in Nepal I had ever seen. But the air went out of me that fifth day in Calcutta—even though I pushed the incident to the back of my mind. I had to make a truce with my memory so that I could sleep at night and not see that man on the ground. I *was* able to process, however, that my American concept of the real world, however valid, had been exposed. The worldview through which I operated was too small and perhaps too misleading to gain an authentic sense of God's working in the world.

There are probably many reasons I failed to act in a Christlike manner that fifth day in Calcutta. One of them had to do with my capacity to see from a Kingdom perspective. I was no missionary at that time, and my faith was not mature enough to imagine a godly response. Still, the image of that man haunted me all through my term as a graduate student at Yale, and I hated the sense of powerlessness it would conjure within me. In 1982, the second year of my master's degree program, God used my India experience to direct me to join a Christian nonprofit organization in Los Angeles that was seeking to empower the poor. I wanted to learn; I wanted another chance to be more than a sympathetic bystander. I wanted to be an agent of change.

Two years later, I moved from South Central Los Angeles to the poorest street I could find in Orange County and started InnerCHANGE.

Years later, after I had stopped an intense gang fight by stepping into the action and commanding the violence to stop in the name of God, I realized what I should have done in India. I should have lain over the beggar being beaten. It was the only thing I could have done, given who I was as an outsider. But I failed to see this at the time.

The reasons that I failed to see authentically and to act redemptively that fifth day in Calcutta are, in many ways, my motive for writing this book. I set out to see poverty in India and came face-to-face with poor people instead. Despite my good intentions to personally observe and respond in India, I was at best a ministry tourist. I had not taken the time to learn the language, culture and history. Equally important, I had not acquired this knowledge from the poor themselves. I had not submerged myself as Jesus had submerged Himself in our world through His incarnation. Good intentions, I found, were not enough.

In Calcutta, I also saw the need for essential character formation, not simply skills training. The reason I failed to act as a Good Samaritan for the beggar on the ground was not just that I didn't know enough, but that I was a beggar spiritually. Likewise, as I reflected on Christ's parable of the Good Samaritan, I realized that the reason the priest and the Levite did not stop for the wounded man had little to do with not knowing enough. These two men were steeped in spiritual tradition and the theology of the day. If I understand Jesus' story rightly, the failure of the first two passersby was a failure of character and emotional strength.

In my Calcutta encounter, I saw the need to develop mission workers among the poor whose priorities were spiritual and emotional growth. My experience helped me to confront the reality of Psalm 51:6: that there were hidden places in my "inmost being" to which God desired to bring truth and wisdom. The traditional religious orders and their focus on learning that *forms*, not simply *informs*, were important models to appraise as I journeyed forward.

Finally, my time in Calcutta taught me how important it is to journey with committed others. It is always a privilege to live and work among the poor; it doesn't always feel like it, however. In bonding among the needy, we often find ourselves steering along the jagged edge of people's fractured lives—and sometimes we discover that the fractures within *us* are the sharpest and most acute. Again, religious orders seemed a good model to consider for going deep in the journey with Jesus among the poor. As I looked at the history of orders that worked among the poor, I detected that their members did not merely survive; they seemed to thrive. Certainly many were able to sustain long-term, even lifetime, commitments to one another in rigorous mission among the poor. Their lives recall the wisdom of an ancient Swedish proverb: Shared joy is double joy; shared sorrow is half sorrow. We have found this to be true, that joined in committed community we are better able to bear losses and authentically celebrate victories.

beyond analysis

We have to understand that the world can only be grasped by action,
not by contemplation. The hand is more important than the eye. . . .
The hand is the cutting edge of the mind.

JACOB BRONOWSKI

In the summer of 1986, I was invited to the home of a long-established, affluent Los Angeles lawyer, in his eighties, who had expressed interest in supporting ministry among the poor. InnerCHANGE's work in Orange County—about an hour south of Los Angeles—on Minnie Street, the poorest, most overcrowded street, was only 18 months old then. We numbered three full-time members and dozens of volunteers in a fascinating three-block world composed primarily of Cambodian refugees and recent Latino immigrants. Minnie Street was so dangerous at that point, with the crack trade ramping up and as many as five gangs competing over that turf, that I was the only one of our number who was actually living there.

This lawyer, whom I will call Reed, lived in exclusive Hancock Park, an area of turn-of-the-century Los Angeles mansions, broad boulevards, big shade trees and old money. Over an elegant dinner served on his terrace, he spoke expansively about Los Angeles, especially about its past. He recalled buckboard driving on Melrose when it was still a dirt track. Lionel Barrymore had been a friend and client, along with other silent-screen stars. He had a great love for the city.

On the Edge

As twilight moved in, I gently steered the conversation to the city's present. Reed settled in his chair and took in the whispering water of his marble fountain with the satisfaction of a classic film producer. In fact, the ambience was so tranquil that I was nearly compelled to say something soothing about inner-city Los Angeles for a man who had invested emotionally in the city's glamorous image.

Instead, I confided that Los Angeles and Orange County were desperate at the core, and that people were on the edge.

"What edge?" he asked.

"The edge of despair and rage," I replied.

I sketched out what was happening in the inner city, emphasizing how state and federal programs had essentially pursued a policy of containment, doing just enough in the inner cities to check the advance of drugs and gangs into the suburbs.

Reed shifted uncomfortably in his chair, and I asked him to envision another kind of effort—a holistic effort that was spiritual at its center. This effort would work to serve, not merely to provide services. It would be a ministry that followed Christ's incarnational model and would be willing to commit to sending teams of carefully prepared missionaries into the most blighted of inner city blocks, taking Christ at His word to drop like grains of wheat into the ground (see John 12:24).

Reed was taken aback that I would propose that Christian workers should actually relocate among the poor. He was all for ministry *to* the poor but not *among* them. He then recounted efforts he had supported, how he had purchased clothes, schoolbooks, pencils, and so on. I agreed that these were necessary things but, in the end, they were still just things. "People change people," I said, trying not to preach. I was painfully aware that I was a 31-year-old man addressing a man who had seen much more of life than I had. Nevertheless, I told Reed that if the church did not seize the opportunity to invest its people among the poor and present living models of good news in both word and works, then eventually, problems festering in inner cities would spill over into the suburban and more affluent neighborhoods. "If we don't pay now, then we'll have to pay later," I warned. "And time will simply raise the price."

About that time, Reed looked around at his high stone walls. Nearly 50 years of living peacefully in his home kept him from visualizing people from the inner city storming his ramparts. We were coming from different perspectives, and we knew it.

While driving home to Minnie Street later that evening, I couldn't shake the image of Reed sitting comfortably in his lawn chair, not knowing that only a few miles away, in downtown Los Angeles, thousands were scavenging in bins for leftovers while others scraped together enough money for a hit to take the edge off the night. I wondered if Reed's vision for the poor of L.A., telescoped through a series of black-tie benevolences, would be enlarged if he could accompany me on a midnight journey through the Garment District. Would he change his perspective if he could see the thousands of homeless, sleeping in rows in coffin-shaped appliance boxes?

I never saw Reed again, although we spoke once on the phone. He died about a year after our dinner, so he never saw Los Angeles erupt into the rioting that would become the worst civil disturbance in the United States in the twentieth century. And he never saw the riots spill over into neighborhoods like his.

When the Lid Blew Off

In the spring of 1992, the riots swept through Los Angeles with a speed and fury that caught everyone off guard. My wife, Deanna, and I had recently moved from Minnie Street into an apartment complex with 300 or more Cambodian refugees in a rough area of Long Beach (west of Santa Ana, in Los Angeles County)—an area that combined low-income blacks, whites and Latinos. Even in the best of times, there was an uneasy truce between these groups.

On the second day that the riots raged in Los Angeles, just before they overran Long Beach, there was an eerie quiet in our neighborhood. Deanna and I sat Cambodian-style on the floor of our front room, praying that God would protect Long Beach. But as the sun slid down toward the horizon, plumes of smoke wafted up over the Pacific Coast Highway, less than half a mile away. We joined a group of our neighbors on the roof and scanned the skyline. Soon fires were in front of us, to the left of us and just behind us. We heard the shattering sound of metal on glass and knew our corner stores were being looted.

Rioters began streaming down our street with armloads of merchandise, some with bags as big as Santa Claus's. Together with a little knot of our neighbors, we drifted down toward our front gate, almost in a daze. Suddenly a car sped past and one of its passengers hurled a full beer can, which hit one of us in the chest. That was all it took for our neighbors to rush into their apartments and emerge with guns.

These were men who had lost homes, possessions and family members in Cambodia to the Khmer Rouge, and they were not about to lose anyone or anything again. Some began patrolling the perimeter, others the rooftops. In a moment, our peaceful complex was transformed into a paramilitary camp. Deanna and I had lived in the complex for only a few months, but in that time we had developed enough relationships to calm our neighbors and persuade the men to come down from their provocative positions on the roofs.

The lens of crisis yields a strange and sharpened vision. I still remember it all clearly: the color of the sky; where we stood in the middle of the courtyard; Paul, a dear man and our "village elder," running down the middle staircase, barking directions to huddled groups of neighbors. Din followed, self-consciously carrying an automatic weapon. Aht trundled behind, wearing an anxious expression. Deanna and I assured them we would pray that God would calm our city, and we admonished them to keep vigil inside our apartment complex. Even more than the physical scene, what I most keenly recall is a sense, a flicker, really, that we were exactly where we were supposed to be; that the random, split-ended way I normally governed my life came together in the certain thread of destiny. We were engaged in work that God had prepared for us before the foundation of the world.

Late that evening, on television, city officials remarked on the tremendous cost, in the millions of dollars, of keeping additional law enforcement officers on duty. In the crucible of those few days, I remembered my past conversation with Reed, and the Church's missed opportunity came to me in a rush of regret. How much cheaper and more effective would it have been to have planted transforming Christian communities in our inner cities to work for lasting spiritual change from the inside out? Instead, we had simply followed our government's lead in a policy of containment.

A Sermon and a Fine Dusting of Ashes

The following Sunday, May 3, 1992, the day after most of the rioting ended, Deanna and I dressed for church, stepped out into the Southern California glare and walked briskly to our car. It was a morning like any other spring morning in the Long Beach area, except that there was still tension in the air and a fine dusting of ash on our windshield.

Normally, Deanna and I attended a small Cambodian church, but that Sunday we headed toward one of the largest, most influential mainstream churches in the area to see how it would respond to the riots. On the way, we surveyed the wreckage. A few buildings still smoldered. Scavengers picked their way through Thursday night's rubble that had cooled. At one corner, I asked Deanna to stop the car. I remember looking at the destruction and thinking, *How did it all come to this?* Never before had I seen the gap between the American Dream and the American Fact illustrated so profoundly.

That morning, the pastor delivered a blistering sermon on American culture. He said that American culture was sinking toward the sunset, that we lived increasingly in a post-Christian age, and that we must stop confusing Americanism with Christianity. He affirmed what newscasters had said all week, that the riots were a wake-up call for the city. But more than that, he said they were a wake-up call for the people of God. Then he paused and said, "We must be biblical in our diagnosis or we'll see no solution."

Years later, I still remember that sermon. I sympathized with its message. I agreed that we needed a biblical diagnosis. But something troubled me about the analysis the pastor gave that Sunday and all the other analyses we heard that week and for weeks afterward. We never seemed to get beyond the analysis to the solution.

Years later, with the smell of smoke gone, the wake-up call appears to be gone too. It's as if everyone hit the snooze button. I don't disagree with the analyses themselves. Many captured some critical insights for change. My problem is with society's and the Church's captivation with the process. Analyses begot more analyses and ultimately begot blame. There is nothing that stops forward movement toward transformation as much as blame.

During the riots and immediately afterward, everyone's eyes were on Los Angeles. Everyone, it seemed, had an analysis to offer and someone to blame. Some saw the riots as a backlash against prejudice. Others saw them as reverse discrimination. Some cried injustice. Others saw ingratitude as the culprit. Some saw the riots as the final shudder of a moribund welfare system. Others blamed the legacy of the 1980s style of trickle-down politics and economics.

Analysis Paralysis

Two thousand years ago, Jesus confronted this same inclination to find blame among His own followers. In the Gospel of John, in the story of how Christ healed a man blind from birth, the disciples asked, "Rabbi, who sinned, this man or his parents, that he was born blind?" (John 9:2). Immediately the disciples began to analyze and seek blame. Rather than ask Jesus what they could do to help, they detached themselves by asking why he was blind. But Jesus responded, "Neither this man nor his parents sinned; he was born blind so that God's works might be revealed in him" (v. 3).

Jesus sidestepped the counterfeit debate and recast the negative scenario as one of hopeful opportunity. The issue, He said, was neither the man nor his parents; the issue was that God wanted to reveal His power in the blind man. It is curious that in this third and final year of His ministry when the disciples had walked so many miles with Jesus and had seen Him heal so many, their first impulse was to analyze and seek blame. For them the blind man was a problem to ponder or, worse, a misfortune to move away from lest he be contagious.

Jesus was, and is, so different. He simply reached out and touched the man. It was embarrassingly simple: Jesus acted.

Christ committed Himself to a ministry of compassionate presence, not dispassionate distance. He showed that the tragedies of the world are not first to be reasoned, but treated.

Back to the riots. It took four days and nights for the riots to burn themselves out—all 632 fires. It was uncomfortable to know that history was being made that week and that it was ugly. As terrible as those days were, Deanna and I began to console ourselves with the hope that, surely, the aftermath of the riots would bring an unprecedented outpouring of activity and concern on behalf of the inner-city poor.

As a matter of fact, immediately after the riots, all kinds of people focused on South Central Los Angeles, determined to regain the initiative and make constructive history. They were determined to forge a preferable future that included all Angelinos, both the haves and the have-nots. They pledged themselves not only to repair damage but also, more significantly, to heal injustices and decades of neglect. Local, state and federal officials worked to rally resources to create Enterprise Zones. The unsinkable Peter Ueberroth, the business mogul who so skillfully organized the 1984 Summer Olympic Games in Los Angeles, was placed in charge of the rebuilding and "bridge building." But a year later, with the crisis in remission, he resigned. The pledged money had only partially come in, and most of the volunteers had long since stopped journeying down to South Central to work for change.

It didn't surprise us much that Los Angeles the city rapidly returned to business as usual. What did surprise us was that most churches did too. The initial burst of volunteerism, largely organized around clean-up projects, slowly petered out.

No baton was passed to long-term workers who would relocate and act as church planters, neighborhood mission workers and community organizers. The bridges that were built between suburban and inner-city churches were largely abandoned.

How different history would be if Moses had seen the burning bush, shrugged, and simply walked by, muttering, "My, what a strange meteorological formation." The riots were more than a wake-up call for the Church in the city of Los Angeles. They were a "burning bush" experience that offered an opportunity to step off the normal path and write a new redemptive history weaving suburban and urban Christians together. Yet the Church, with only a few exceptions, walked by, and the unique opportunity to forge a more holistic, urban/suburban vision and raise up new workers who would sub-merge, connecting with the poor and oppressed, passed.

Caught Up in Autobiography

There are a number of reasons why Christians failed to help write a more redemptive, wider spread, just history at this particular moment of opportunity. A lack of visionary leadership on the heels of the multiple analyses was part of the problem. I believe that genuinely concerned Christians in the greater Los Angeles area simply did not know what to do or how to do it. Church training programs primarily continue to raise up pastoral leaders and a few missional leaders who consider the city their parish. Fifty to 60 years ago, when churches were still neighborhood congregations and exerted parish influence, they were committed to the welfare of a micro-community. But with the rise of commuter life and specifically the commuter church, parish influence on a micro-level has broken down, especially in a large city like Los Angeles. It has not been replaced by macro-vigilance and influence. When something like the riots cuts a devastating swath through the city, the Church finds itself with neither the clout to reclaim turf block by block nor the influence to lead and organize renewal on a citywide level.

Another reason why I believe this opportunity to write redemptive history among the poor passed us by is that we Christians in Los Angeles, and in many churches in the prosperous Western world, are generally caught up in our autobiographies. We are fully invested in our own over-scheduled lives. And we have made it difficult to retreat from these driven lives because we have come to construe them as normal.

Jesus addressed the problem of an all-consuming "autobiography"—the pursuit of a material agenda at the cost of our faith—in His parable of the rich fool who speculates on how he can retain more earnings with bigger barns:

> Then He told them a parable: "The ground of a certain rich man produced a good crop. He thought to himself, 'What shall I do? I have no place to store my crops.' Then he said, 'This is what I'll do. I will tear down my barns and build bigger ones, and there I will store all my grain and my goods. And I'll say to myself, "You have plenty of good things laid up for many years. Take life easy; eat, drink and be merry."' But God said to him, 'You fool! This very night your life will be demanded from you. Then who will get what you have prepared

for yourself?' This is how it will be with anyone who stores up things for himself but is not rich toward God." (Luke 12:16-21)

This parable describes the quintessential self-made man. Except for the rural imagery, Jesus could be describing the twenty-first-century consumer dream. We must give this man his due. He came by all his money honestly. The parable tells us that his land was very productive, and through a combination of shrewd investments, good portfolio management and perhaps good luck, he multiplied his assets to such a degree that even his creative retirement funds couldn't contain his wealth. Today, Wall Street would call him a good businessman. Perhaps admirers would line up to attend his seminars and discover his steps to success.

This man pictured himself growing old in style and comfort—with a putting green, a climate-controlled wine cellar and an entertainment center—all the while humming the ballad Frank Sinatra made famous with the words "I did it my way." But let's not miss an important detail in verse 17 of this parable. When the rich man spoke, he was not speaking to his wife, his broker or his closest friend, let alone to God. He was speaking to himself. Here again Jesus' parable rings true to life in that too much money often isolates. Excess can undermine dependence on God and others and bring on the terminal disease of loneliness. This man did not talk with God, because he did not have God on his mind, let alone his needy neighbors.

Of course, we can also read the Parable of the Talents (Matt. 25-14-30), and we can see God at work in the marketplace today.

But the point here is that the excessive pursuit of wealth can crowd out the single-minded pursuit of Jesus.

The World Pulled Down over Our Eyes

Our culture tends to celebrate people like the man in the parable and commend their scramble to the top. In the United States, we tolerate a gap between rich and poor where CEOs of large firms average $10 million a year—compensation 370 times greater than that of the average hourly worker.[7] As Christians, we must ask ourselves, Is this the world we want to live in?

Certainly many Christians would conclude that the rich fool in the parable struggled with greed, and they would privately advise him to give some money away. But a disturbing number among us would agree with the world that this man was a sharp businessperson. Many churches would affirm him as a good steward.

Robert Wuthnow, a man who has spent much of his life studying the Church in the United States, discovered in the late 1990s that only 3 percent of Christians discuss their incomes with other Christians, and only 4 percent are willing to talk about their money with their pastors.[8] Obviously, money management is a sensitive issue, but with so little accountability, many of us set about building bigger barns rather than investing in the Kingdom. American Christians began the new millennium giving only about 2.6 percent of their incomes to charity, just a percentage point above non-Christians, who averaged about 1.6 percent.[9]

The world might call this man a good businessperson; the church might call him a good steward. But Jesus said to him, "You fool." Money has its own gravitational pull. Jesus warns, "Take care! Be on your guard against all kinds of greed; for one's life does not consist in the abundance of possessions" (Luke 12:15).

In 1985, I watched crack invade Minnie Street and reduce lives to something to be measured in fractions of grams. Substance abuse took more lives in those days than I care to recall. But when I consider the eternal consequences of a "substance" like money—that it is easier for a camel to pass through the eye of a needle than for a rich person to enter the Kingdom—I wonder if we need to redefine substance abuse.

There is a saying: Greed can never get enough; worry is afraid it will never have enough. After finishing the story of the rich fool, Jesus continues in verses 22 and 23 to clarify that not only greed but also anxiety about security can undo us. "Therefore I tell you, do not worry about your life, what you will eat; or about your body, what you will wear. Life is more than food, and the body more than clothes." Suddenly we see that Jesus is not simply addressing those of us who succumb to greed; He is also addressing those of us who build bigger barns for financial reassurance.

When Jesus asks us in verse 27 to consider the splendor of the lilies, He is not calling us to live in any other way except abundantly. He invites us into a fullness and significance that can come only from seeking the Kingdom first. This Kingdom is so fair, so full, that Jesus tells us its single-minded pursuit will bring into alignment all other needs, all other holy grails.

Where are we investing our lives today? In a culture that proclaims that greed is good and that exhorts us to muster the courage to be rich, it is easy to lose our way chasing wealth and justify it later as responsible living.

Urban Nocturne: A Journey Back to the Street

Many years have passed since I lived in Orange County.

It is evening. I turn right onto Minnie Street. I feel like I am in a canyon, and the gathering darkness adds to the sensation. Two-story apartment blocks flank the street on either side. Each is horseshoe-shaped around a small courtyard. Some complexes are gated; nearly all need paint and repair.

Once planted with trees and grass, the courtyards are paved now. Cheap stucco peels off their walls. The sounds of children running and yelling bounce back and forth in shattering ricochets. Halfway up the street, the sidewalks teem with people hanging out. I scan the Asian and Latino faces. A few look back at me, curious to see a white man in what is obviously a rented car driving slowly down a street he would have to be lost to find. But I am not lost; I am returning.

Near the end of Minnie Street, I turn left into an alley and cruise a back parking lot. As wide as a soccer field and twice as long, the lot is filled with big, older model cars. Some sit partially stripped, but there are more cars in good condition now than there were 10 years ago. On my left, a dealer signals to me with his cigarette hand, the orange glow making shooting star patterns in the dark. On my right, a prostitute slinks between parked cars. Back walls are mosaics of graffiti. Broken glass ground into the asphalt gleams like stardust in my headlights.

I do a U-turn in the parking lot and return to Minnie Street. When I get to #825, I catch a glimpse of Apphai and start to pull over. But it is not Apphai—he would be nearly 20 now. Suddenly the images come fast and furious. In my mind's eye, I see Sakharini running to meet me, his brother close behind. Chit, Sith and Sophal practice slam-dunking on an eight-foot, makeshift basket in the space between buildings. Emotion rises within me, and I know that if I don't move on, I really will start crying.

Minnie Street was my address for seven years. It was on this street that I started InnerCHANGE. It was here that we first dreamed of sending a team to Cambodia. Minnie Street acted as an anvil on which we could hammer our faith and clarify that intimacy with God was essential to our mission. This was a street that trusted us, forgave us our failures and embraced us as its own. Did we need to live there to see Christ facilitate transformation in that neighborhood and see more than 100 persons come to Christ? Could a church have been planted, youth and children's clubs founded, basketball leagues organized, and gang members reconciled had we not made Minnie Street our home and pursued an inside-out empowerment strategy? Could we not have just commuted to this Santa Ana street, avoided the personal cost and minimized the danger? Moreover, *should* we have lived apart from Minnie Street, retained addresses elsewhere and instead channeled valuable energies devoted to learning language and culture toward mobilizing resources to engage poverty at a more macro level?

Dropping like grains of wheat into the ground and growing up in the cultures of Minnie Street, allowing ourselves to be drawn into the intricate web of relationships—all this was time consuming. Could our impact have been quicker and greater had we simply brokered our resources and leveraged connections in an outside-in strategy?

These are fair questions to ask.

Living incarnationally among the poor has always been controversial. On the one hand, those who have shared lives with the poor, like Francis of Assisi, Dorothy Day and Mother Teresa, have been fiercely admired. But incarnational workers among the poor have also been ridiculed and condemned for exposing their lives and those of their children to the dangerous conditions of the poor. Furthermore, the scale and speed of our work have been troubling to some who are more accustomed to quick returns on investments.

Many of us have encountered this split response from mainstream believers. We have been affirmed as "real Christians" and have been lauded for our radical expression of Christ's presence among the poor. But some of our dearest friends have also confided to us that they consider us a little unhinged or, worse, irresponsible. Several years ago, while living and ministering in San Francisco, Deanna and I were closely questioned for our decision to enroll our girls in an inner-city school in a city reputed to have the worst-run public school system in California. When Deanna and I contemplated a move to Cambodia with our infant daughter, one of my friends exploded, "That has to be a sin! It can't be right to take a baby to a country as poor as Cambodia."

Is incarnational ministry worth the risk? Is it worth the price to sub-merge—to leave what is known and comfortable behind? Are the returns gratifying enough to continue to invest in an inside-out strategy and call others to that model? I have often asked myself these questions when the rigors of living in a poor neighborhood mount and the returns seem far away. For my family and me, these are the most personal of questions, and they have no short or easy answers.

I knew much disappointment on Minnie Street. There were fewer powerful New Testament moments than I'd hoped for. Many people we loved did not come to the faith. On the other hand, I learned to strive less and fret less about out-

Yolanda's Story
Deanna Hayes

It was an ordinary day. The sun was shining, and the fervent pace of San Francisco stretched residents to their usual capacities—working, traveling, hurrying. Savannah and I strode casually along, passing through the tall white gates of the Valencia Gardens Housing Development. We had no agenda that day, just a visit to neighbors whose lives were beleaguered by the complexities of poverty. Hand in hand we entered the long courtyard of concrete paths, sparse trees and low brick walls painted Easter bunny pink.

Shots rang out. A woman grabbed her young daughter, threw her to the pavement and dove on top of her. Burning rubber screamed the departure of the speeding car, and then for a moment, silence.

comes. More important, while living among the poor, I experienced unexpected moments of fullness that were like tide pools teeming with fragile meaning.

Night Is Coming

Deanna and I have tried to cultivate in ourselves and in Inner-CHANGE a bias toward action. That bias has taken us to the edge many times. It has also committed us, at times, to obscure places far beyond the mainstream's field of vision.

Discerning God's lead while at the brink of decision can be challenging. Not all of my decisions to act have been wise ones.

The toddler's innocent, peaceful play shattered into uncontrollable sobs blending with the screams and tears of her mother. Sirens shrieked the arrival of the police as a young man bled on the sidewalk. Another drug deal, another reality check of inner-city life.

Violence is not new to me. I have walked unwittingly into gunfire on city streets and have stood two feet from my husband as a gun was held to his head. But this was different. My most precious gift was clenched beside me, her hand in mine.

Usually I unabashedly embrace an I-can-bear-almost-anything attitude. Yet there is one road I have begged God never to take me down—losing one of my children. I'm not sure that I could bear it, and for that one moment in a typical afternoon, my faith was tested to its maximum capacity. Is incarnational ministry worth the risk? Is it worth the price to sub-merge? My answer is Yolanda.

But I know this: Jesus of the Gospels is more committed to action than I comfortably admit. When I stop to tally my regrets, I can think of fewer than a handful of times when I acted prematurely. On the other hand, I can recall numerous times when I stayed on the sidelines as an opportunity slipped away. "We must do the works of Him who sent us," Jesus reminds me, "as long as it is day. Night is coming, when no one can work." (see John 9:4).

There is also good news. In the aftermath of the Cold War, the world entered a period of unprecedented political and economic freedom. During the 1990s, globalization stimulated growth in much of the developing world at three times the

I have two natural daughters, but I consider Yolanda my third daughter. Yolanda grew up in Valencia Gardens. From infancy, she has been engulfed by the burdens of poverty. Abandoned by her natural father, she became fatherless again when her stepfather was killed in New Year's Eve violence. Yolanda was reared in the housing projects on welfare by a courageous mom who also protectively shepherded numbers of other neighborhood kids.

Yolanda is different from most inner-city youth stereotyped in police dramas and highlighted in the crime section of city newspapers. In high school, while her peers partied, dropped out of school, became unwed mothers or ended up in jail, Yolanda became a Christian and a different model for those who knew her. When a young girl on the dance team Yolanda coached started failing classes and ran away from home, Yolanda took her into her own bedroom, signed her up for summer school and made sure she got to and from school each day.

growth rate of the industrial world in its heyday in the nine-teenth century. In the last quarter of the twentieth century, life expectancy at birth rose from 55 to 67 years. In roughly the same period, infant mortality in the two-thirds world dropped by half.[10] Jeffrey Sachs, author of *The End of Poverty*, cites recent statistics to indicate that extreme poverty (those living on $1 a day or less) is declining worldwide, both in absolute numbers and as a percentage of population.[11]

Unfortunately, in some of the most vulnerable parts of the developing world, progress from globalization has come at a high price. Many of the traditional family and kinship networks that provide a safety net for the poor have begun to break down.

Had I not been willing to take risks and build a life in parts of the city where others refused to walk, I would have missed the privilege of inspiring a young woman who has the qualities to transform—and who is transforming—the world around her. ✳

Yolanda

Consequently, even as they have decreased in number proportionally in terms of total population, the needy have come to live more precarious lives. Brazil is a good example of a country whose surging growth has come with collateral social cost. In 1962 there were about 2.5 million abandoned children roaming Brazil's streets. Now it is estimated there are as many as 8 million.[12] Another example of the deterioration of family networks can be seen in the rise of prostitution. It has been estimated that between 700,000 and 4 million people, mostly women and girls, are sold or lured into the commercial sex trade each year.[13]

Christians throughout the world can no longer claim ignorance about the plight of the poor. Modern media keep us posted on the miseries of the needy worldwide. As followers of Jesus, we *know* that we are on the road to Jericho described by the parable of the Good Samaritan. Irish rock star Bono has noted that we no longer live in a world in which distance determines who our neighbor is. We have glimpsed the world's needy who are battered by the system and left by the wayside. But even with the multiple opportunities to engage the poor in our increasingly interconnected world, too often we still hurry by the poor. They exist in our spiritual blind spot. Too late, their images register in our rearview mirror of guilt. Our problem with the Good Samaritan parable is not in Jesus' definition of a good neighbor. Our problem, in a shallow world of low commitment and lower follow-through, is in exercising His command, "Go and do likewise" (Luke 10:37).

This statistical portrait of the *real* real world can be more numbing than motivating. This touches on an essential problem. We've seen poverty up close in the West on TV, in the news and driving by our inner cities. Moreover, some of us who have not experienced poverty have at least measured it, studied it or analyzed it. Poverty, we know about. It's poor people we do not know; but it's *knowing* poor people that enables substantive change and authentic empowerment to take place.

Yet the statistics of poverty are so overwhelming, especially when considered globally, that we either succumb to overexposure or tend to gravitate toward large-scale solutions, projects and programs. Critical relational strategies that could give precision to these macro strategies appear to take too much time, have too little short-term payoff and invite personal burnout. So when it comes to connecting with poor people, actually getting down off one's donkey seems unrealistic.

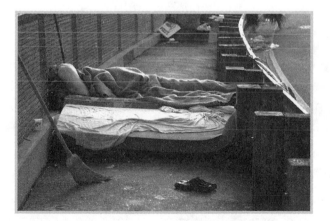

CHAPTER 3

no poor in the land

No one was born to be a slave or a beggar. No one.

DOM HELDER CAMERA

Growing up the first 12 years of my life in small towns in Pennsylvania, Kansas, Tennessee and Colorado, it didn't seem to matter that we were lower middle-class in our lifestyle, that we were five, six, ultimately seven people crowding into small, two-bedroom houses, often in the marginal parts of town. Most of the students we went to school with in the late 1950s and early 1960s were doing only somewhat better. It was the rare family that had the new suburban tract home complete with two-car garage, back patio and sliding glass door.

Our economic status didn't really matter to me until we moved to Albuquerque, a big city in New Mexico, and I entered junior high school. Money was always tight for us, but at this time, my father decided to pursue a Ph.D. in physics, further shrinking his teacher's hours and salary.

As usual, we were pressed into a box of a house in a mild state of disrepair. I can still remember where the linoleum had peeled away or was coming up on the kitchen floor, because it was my job to wash the floors. I can recall the fly-swatter slam of our back screen door, inexpertly hung, looking out onto our cracked concrete patio. My two sisters slept with my baby brother in the dining room, and my brother, Matt, and I slept in a bedroom the size of a large hallway. We often bought our bread day-old, our clothes secondhand, and many of our furnishings from Goodwill. Nothing was brand name. It wasn't an easy place to bring friends home to.

To make matters worse, our house was next door to the one nice house on the block. Mrs. Teitsel's house was like a Laura Ashley cottage. Even her flowers were color-coordinated. Her front lawn was manicured like a putting green. Ours, on the other hand, looked like a sand trap.

The first year, seventh grade, wasn't too bad in Albuquerque, because I went to public school. In the eighth grade, I received a scholarship to attend an exclusive private school on the wealthy side of town. Suddenly my teenage ego began to keep score as I compared my lifestyle against that of my friends. I can't remember one classmate who didn't have his own bedroom. Vacations came, and my friends traveled to Vail or Aspen to ski. During summers, they went to holiday homes, tennis camp and played golf. My family took low-budget camping trips.

My best friend dropped by one day and insisted on seeing my room. While my face drained of color, he pushed his way

A Tale of Two Worlds

David Eldridge, Melbourne, Australia

I am sitting on a wooden bench, splinters sticking into my bottom. With me are a group of students with their chicken burgers, nachos and fancy shrink-wrapped sandwiches. I sit there explaining that I am not hungry. For me, buying something to eat is a luxury.

Thankfully, I am saved from embarrassment by the social etiquette that you do not bring a cut lunch to school. The reality is that I don't have any food at home either. I couldn't bring a cut lunch and go sit in a corner somewhere, alone, even if I wanted to. So I sit here with the other students, yet still alone—a part of what is going on and yet not a part.

I listen to the small talk, thinking that is just what it is, small talk—which mobile phone to buy, what computer to upgrade to, where to go on their holidays at the end of the year. I, on the other hand, am wondering when I am next going to eat and whether I will get home that night on the train without getting caught by the train inspectors for not having a ticket.

They are planning on what they're going to do for the rest of their lives. Their talk is optimistic. They think about tomorrow. I am planning for how to get through the rest of the day. My thoughts are fatalistic. I do not think about tomorrow.

There is no highlighting the fact that I am not eating again, no drawing of attention, no shout from the rooftop. But I know. I know that the basic needs and concerns of my life and theirs are totally different. I am surrounded by people yet feel totally alone, isolated in a world of people, alienated by my own needs.

I work to belong in their world but am separated by the film wrap that surrounds their sandwiches. That barrier looks easy to break through and yet is remarkably effective in keeping out alien and unwanted matter like me.

They are in their world, I am in mine, and never the twain shall meet. *

past me and proceeded to inspect our entire house. By the time he ducked under the spare clothesline stretched across the kitchen, he pronounced our home an "Okie farm."

In my freshman year, I tried out for the basketball team but suddenly realized I had a crisis on my hands. We practiced after school, so trying out for basketball meant taking the late bus home. But there was no late bus on Fridays. Students arranged their own transportation. Most were picked up by their parents or drove their own cars. My dad couldn't take the time to go all the way to the school, and my mother didn't drive. So I had to get a ride home with an older boy who had a car.

Friday evening came. I was riding with Dave, when halfway home it hit me—he's going to see my house. What if he wants to come in? In a moment of panic, I directed him to a nicer neighborhood several blocks away, telling him that I had to mow a lawn there. Dave gave me an odd look—the sun had just gone down—but he dropped me off, threw his car into gear and waved good-bye.

I watched him turn the corner, picked up my books and started the long walk home—one of the most miserable walks I ever took. On the way, I resolved never again to betray my family over a little embarrassment on account of our living conditions.

Compared to the suffering we have seen as members of InnerCHANGE in the developing world, my miserable embarrassment that evening in the presence of my friend was slight. We were not poor, and furthermore, my parents gave us advantages other children did not receive. But under the magnifying glass of teenage sensitivity, the shame was huge. I share this story to illustrate the fact that in our world, shame and poverty all too often go together.

Yet where in the Bible does it say that the person who is poor should be ashamed just for being poor? We know that the apostle Paul admonishes the poor who will not work (see 2 Thess. 3:10), and certainly those who are not working have reason to avoid eye contact. But for the poor who are squeezed in an unjust system, dispossessed or marginalized—the overwhelming majority of the poor, both biblically and in our world today—where does it say their poverty should be covered in disgrace? In fact, the message of the gospel is just the opposite. James wrote, "But let the brother of humble circumstances glory in his high position; and let the rich man glory in his humiliation, because like flowering grass he will pass away" (1:9-10, *NASB*).

Valley of Dry Bones
Diane Moss, Cambodia

Ezekiel 37:1-6:

> The hand of the Lord was upon me, and he brought me out by the Spirit of the Lord and set me in the middle of a valley; it was full of bones. He led me back and forth among them, and I saw a great many bones on the floor of the valley, bones that were very dry. He asked me, "Son of man, can these bones live?" I said, "O Sovereign Lord, you alone know." Then he said to me, "Prophesy to these bones and say to them, 'Dry bones, hear the word of the Lord! This is what the Sovereign Lord says to these bones: I will make breath enter you, and you will come to life. I will attach tendons to you and make flesh come upon you and cover you with skin; I will

"Humiliation" is a powerful word. How many affluent people consider their wealth a "humiliation"? In contrast, how many poor people glory in their "high position"? I suspect that around the world we can find few poor, even Christian poor, who regard their status with pride. Yet God's word is so emphatic in the book of James. This passage is only one example of an idea that runs all through the central nervous system of Scripture: The kingdom of God is upside-down compared to the world. Again, in the Beatitudes (see Matt. 5), Jesus inverts our hierarchies by saying that the Kingdom is about the weak and the poor being blessed, the last being first, so that everyone can see that we have an affirmative-action God

put breath in you, and you will come to life. Then you will know that I am the Lord.

Valleys are not the places we usually choose. Generally, we're more mountaintop people.

Weighing barely 50 pounds, 26-year-old Srim Pean was hardly more than bones when we found her. She had been laid in the valley, so to speak, cast behind the door of her mother's thatched hut. Behind the door, Pean was blocked from the family's sight and, consequently, blocked from their hearts as well. We carried Pean out and wedged her body on a small motorcycle between two staff members from Sunrise Hospice. She lived at our hospice for more than four months and began taking ARVs (antiretroviral medications). We spoke God's words to her through our prayers, meals and loving physical care. When Pean left us, she was reborn in the Lord. She had recovered to nearly the average weight of a young Khmer woman.

who is personally concerned to redress imbalances.

In our work, we believe Christ when He proclaims, "Blessed are you who are poor, for yours is the kingdom of God" (Luke 6:20). However, we do not romanticize the poor or sentimentalize poverty. As talk show host Jack Paar is quoted as saying, "Poor people have more fun than rich people, they say; I notice that it's the rich people who keep saying it." Neither do we join with those who imply that poverty might somehow mysteriously excuse people for not knowing Christ. Poverty has spiritual benefits, but in and of itself, it cannot redeem. We do not believe that God makes the poor His first concern because they are in some way "best." We have lived long enough among the

Here at Sunrise—Inner-CHANGE's HIV/AIDS home-based care and hospice in Kampong Cham, Cambodia—we have the privilege of walking with people during their darkest moments. In many cases, our hospice residents become stronger and are able to return home.

The following is an English translation of the story Pean told about her life after she left our hospice.

When I left Sunrise, I was fat and lived in a thatch house. I sold small things for neighbors to eat but eventually went bankrupt in that business. I sold my thatched house for $15 and went to Phnom Penh with my mother and younger sister. My thought was that I would be able to get work in Phnom Penh and provide for myself and my mother. I began to work in construction with my sister, who was pregnant. Together we earned $2.50 a day. We could live on the construction site, and this money

poor to observe that poor and rich alike struggle with sinfulness before God. We believe that God puts the poor first because the world puts them last.

Aren't We All Poor in Spirit?

"Is it fair for InnerCHANGE to address the needs of the poor exclusively?" "Aren't the rich just as needy spiritually?" "Aren't we all poor in spirit?"

We often hear these questions in mainstream churches when we present our work. The last question seems to sum up the great temptation to conveniently reinterpret passages deal-

helped us to have food. I needed to get to MSF (*Médecins Sans Frontiéres*, or Doctors without Borders, from France) in Kompong Cham to receive my ARVs, and this cost $2 each way for the bus.

When my sister was seven months pregnant, she had to stop working in construction, and that cut our money in half. I was no longer able to travel to KC to get my ARVs. My health began to fail. In my job, I did things like bringing cement up five floors. This hard work caused my health to fail even

Pean

ing with the physically poor to mean the poor in spirit. Thus, we who are not materially poor can qualify for God's special concern and blessing, and at the same time avoid passages about the responsibilities of the rich.

Certainly the Bible identifies a commendable spiritual state called "poor in spirit." Jesus confirms in Matthew's account of the Sermon on the Mount that the poor in spirit are blessed (see Matt. 5:3). David, even after he became a wealthy, powerful king, maintained a lifelong attitude of genuine poverty of spirit that we see reflected in the psalms. But the concepts of "poor" and "poor in spirit" are not interchangeable. Furthermore, the biblical instances referring to the poor in spirit do not begin to equal

more. Finally, the leader at work stopped me from working because I had no energy.

I was afraid to come back to Sunrise. Sunrise had helped me a lot, saved my life, but I hadn't taken care of myself. I was too embarrassed to meet Sunrise staff again. I borrowed the money to call my aunt in Kompong Cham, and she sent my uncle to come and get us all. I lived with them for five days, and my aunt spoke strongly to me about going back to Sunrise. The day I arrived, I was received very well by everyone, and the Sunrise doctor took me to MSF to start getting treatment from them again. After that, I went home, and then the doctor came to get me and wanted me to live in the hospice again. I was so very happy. When I arrived back at the hospice, Diane came out to meet me, picked me up in her arms, carried me in and laid me on a bed. She told me she was very happy to see me and that she had hope for

the thousands of passages that address the materially poor, the oppressed, the hungry, the orphaned, and the foreigner or stranger. We must distinguish what the Bible terms the "poor" from the poor in spirit to maintain the integrity of both themes.

Looking again at James 1:9-10, the apostle refers to brothers and sisters of "humble circumstances." He is definitely talking here about things tangible and material. It is hard to spiritualize this verse and bend it to say that the "poor in spirit" glory in their high position. Similarly, James uses the Greek word *plousios* for the word "rich" in a construction used to describe a person who is rich literally. In the next verse, he elaborates further about the rich man, describing him as one "in

me to get better again, just like I had the first time.

When Pean returned, she was back to just about 50 pounds. She had sores around her mouth, a terrible cough and could barely walk or sit up. In the first month back with us, Pean gained almost 10 pounds. Her mother and younger sister are washing clothes for neighbors and selling vegetables at the local market. ✳

the midst of his pursuits." Clearly, James is talking about a man of means and multiple options.

Passages like this one wreak havoc with personal designer theologies about the poor in spirit. Many Christians struggle with God's fairness in selecting the materially poor to be especially "rich in faith and heirs of the kingdom" (Jas. 2:5). Conversely, many wealthy Christians continue to glide past verses like James 5:1, which says, "Come now, you rich, weep and howl," or Jesus' statement, "Woe to you who are rich, for you have already received your comfort" (Luke 6:24) as a warning for someone else.

Two Concerns

Two major concerns need to be addressed about applying the "poor in spirit" phrase to passages that have been written to comfort or describe the condition of the materially poor.

First, in countries like the U.S. and Australia that struggle mightily with materialism, we should be careful how easily we assign the label "poor in spirit." Too often, we console ourselves that it is the love of money, not money itself, that is the root of all evil. Then in the face of Western affluence today, so pervasive in its influence, we suggest that it is harder to become poor in spirit than it is to be poor in possessions. Perhaps this is why Christ confronted the rich young ruler gently with, "Go, give all your possessions to the poor," not, "Go, learn what it means to be poor in spirit."

Being physically poor is a material reality that should not and cannot be spiritualized away. When we reinterpret biblical passages about the poor to refer to the poor in spirit, we play fast and loose with critical realities and ultimately defraud the poor of the essential truths that God intends to be their great hope and comfort. Hannah's song is a good example of this kind of empowering expression to the poor:

> The Lord makes poor and makes rich;
> he brings low, he also exalts.
> He raises up the poor from the dust;
> he lifts the needy from the ash heap,
> to make them sit with princes and inherit a seat of honor.
> For the pillars of the earth are the Lord's,
> and on them he has set the world (1 Sam. 2:7-8).

In these poignant verses, we see that God does not simply stoop to pity the poor but exalts them. How different His attitude is from that of even our best efforts as Christians to help the poor. Do we allow God to exalt the poor through us? Passages such as James 1:9-10, and Hannah's song, are designed by God to go directly into the bloodstream of those with low self-esteem—the low self-esteem so typically expressed by the poor oppressed by our world. These messages are a critical part of the good news of Jesus Christ, contextualized for the poor, aimed at giving real significance to their suffering and healing to their battered self-image.

Two Mirrors

If the mainstream church spiritualizes key passages written *to* the poor, the needy themselves may do the same, because they often see any institution in mainstream society as a model of "success" and use that model to interpret Scripture. For those ministering among the poor, our mission is not complete without introducing the needy to biblical passages that show how God lifts them up. Not only do the poor need to know that they are not forgotten by God, but even more, they need to know that they are affirmed by Him! They need to know that Jesus Himself identifies with them (see Matt. 25:31-46). If we do not have the courage to enable the poor to see themselves in the mirror of the *Word*, then they will see themselves in the mirror of the *world*, and that is not an uplifting picture. After looking into the world's mirror, the poor can all too easily conclude that it is the rich who are blessed, and thus the poor will do all they can to try to imitate them.

How destructive are low self-esteem issues in blocking the truth? The book of Exodus gives us a strong example. Four hundred years of oppression at the bottom of a powerful empire took a toll on the spirit of the Hebrew people and their ability to recognize good news when it was presented to them. Moses returned to the land of his birth to deliver a message of incredible hope and love direct from the Lord, beginning with: "I will take you as my own people and I will be your God" (Exod. 6:7-8). However, when Moses declared this to the people, "they did not listen to him because of their discouragement and cruel bondage" (v. 9). Similarly, some poor in our communities react to God's good news that He esteems them highly and raises them out of the dust with disbelief.

Cambodian poor, for example, whose Buddhist culture insists that they are poor because they were bad in a former life, struggle to embrace a positive self-image based on biblical truths.

In countries like the U.S. and Australia that have strong national rags-to-riches myths, it can be hard for the poor to let go of cherished cultural images of success. God's affirmation of them as poor can feel like a confirmation that they must remain as they are—impoverished in spirit as well as in material goods.

In our work, we are learning what it means to lead poor men and women to Christ, *including their self-esteem*. Otherwise, their souls may belong to God, but their self-esteem will continue to belong to the world. And that can be the difference between an empowered believer and a disempowered believer. This truth is critical because typically only empowered believers experience the blessing that blesses others and sparks the kind of missional movements we all long to see.

Tough Questions

"Must we who are rich throw up our hands, then, and accept condemnation?" some will ask. We find that for many Western Christians, the issue of money is so highly charged and engenders such guilt that our very presence as mission workers among the poor is experienced as a judgment upon them. Wealthy Christians occasionally get frustrated with us because they infer from our words and lives that their spiritual journeys are second class or, worse, completely disobedient.

Must every wealthy Christian sell all and give to the poor as the rich young ruler was instructed? We believe that in cases like the rich young ruler's, where identity is wrapped up in wealth, Jesus, simply out of mercy, does call some to dethrone possessions and renounce all. He does this that they may "take hold of

Sometimes I Still Miss the Point

Samantha Baker Evens

I arrived at Haight Street, San Francisco, ready to hang out with homeless youth, to be a presence on the street, to love as Jesus loved—or at least that's what I wanted to think I was there to do. As I was walking down the street looking for street kids, a voice called to me from the shade of a storefront. It was a voice I knew, but not one I really wanted to hear.

Paul is one of the old-timers, one of the homeless who came to Haight Street during the 1960s as a hippie and never left. He is drunk, smelly, urinates on himself and remembers little from one minute to the next. Other street people make fun of him, and passersby ignore him. So when he called out to me, I cringed. He wanted to talk, and I wanted to walk on, but I sat down, telling myself I'd stay only a minute. After all, I was there to love homeless youth, not old-timers. I talked a bit with him but constantly scanned the streets. What if one of the street kids saw me with Paul? They all think he is disgusting and might think less of me. Paul, thankfully, did not notice my discomfort but rambled on in stream-of-consciousness style, glad to have someone to listen to him. I listened half-heartedly and was about to stand up to leave when he suddenly turned very serious and said, "Sam, sometimes I'm so lonely I don't know what to do."

Two seconds later, Paul had forgotten he said this, but I will never forget it. It chilled my heart to think that I was so ready to minister to those I deemed worthy, but I could so easily walk by one whom God was clearly drawing me in to care for. Paul was truly unlovable in the eyes of the world, but he was a precious child in the eyes of God.

Jesus could see through externals to love those who looked unlovable: tax collectors, prostitutes, foul-smelling lepers and rich young rulers alike. I am not very good at seeing people the way Jesus saw them, but I'm getting better at it. Paul reminds me that the eyes of God see both the smelly old drunk and the misguided young missionary, and He loves us both despite our external—and internal—appearances. ✳

the life that is truly life" (1 Tim. 6:19). But we know many wealthy Christians whom God blesses with abundance in order to bless others. Zacchaeus is a case in point. He volunteered to give half his wealth to the poor and repay four times any sum he had accumulated fraudulently, and Jesus was so impressed with the integrity of his young faith that He affirmed him (see Luke 19:8-10). Jesus did not tell Zacchaeus that his commitment was not enough.

Wealth, then, is not sin. God is a God of abundance, who delights in seeing His children live abundantly. Riches are, however, a heavy responsibility to steward, given that Jesus says it is harder for a rich man to enter the kingdom of God than for a camel to go through the eye of a needle (see Luke 18:25). Paul spoke unambiguously when he wrote, "Command those who are rich in this present world not to be arrogant nor to put their hope in wealth, which is so uncertain, but to put their hope in God, who richly provides us with everything for our enjoyment. Command them to do good, to be rich in good deeds, and to be generous and willing to share" (1 Tim. 6:17-18).

As clear as these passages are, many still find the magnetic pull of wealth beguiling and will find ways to justify accumulating it from such Scripture. Abraham, Job and other godly Old Testament figures, it can be argued, were all wealthy. Indeed, some go beyond legitimizing the amassing of wealth to suggesting that prosperity is a sign of godliness, faith and God's favor. The prosperity doctrine is an extreme expression of this theology. For those who infer God's favor simply because they have been "blessed" with wealth, however, or for those who would argue that their country's rich natural resources are a sign of God's favor, it is instructive to recall that Judas Iscariot was the disciple given charge of Jesus' ministry's money box (see John 13:29). Judas's example reminds us that being entrusted with a lot of resources is not necessarily a sign of spiritual merit.

Lessons From Traditional Religious Orders

On the other hand, voluntary simplicity is not a sign of God's special favor. It can minimize distraction in our devotion to God and can help us identify with the poor (themes addressed in chapter 5), but we must not congratulate ourselves for pursuing a simpler life—neither should we publicly or privately pride ourselves in serving the poor as pinnacle work in the Kingdom. Many of us who work among the poor have James 1:27 memorized: "Religion that God our Father accepts as pure and faultless is this: to look after orphans and widows in their distress . . ."

Our God is an affirming God, and we can encourage ourselves with this passage. Furthermore, we can comfort and arm ourselves with this truth when others suggest that helping the poor is just "social action" and of dubious value in advancing the Kingdom. However, we must not read into James's passage the sense that our expression of the Body of Christ is somehow the best or only pure religion. There is no room for spiritual arrogance in any form, and we are wise to distinguish between feeling affirmed and feeling prideful.

In *The Rise and Fall of Catholic Religious Orders,* author Patricia Wittberg notes that with Pope Paul VI's emphatic pronouncement in Vatican II that the orders were not a superior form of discipleship, membership immediately began to decline from an all-time high in the early 1960s. According to Wittberg, until that time, candidates for the orders found great incentive in thinking that the orders were a "more perfect" way.[14] We do not want to lift up InnerCHANGE as an order—with our special commitments, rhythms and targeted work among the poor—as the only, the best, or even a better-than form of following Jesus.

It is not surprising that all kinds of attitudes have crusted around something as emotionally freighted as serving the poor. Many attitudes collect around the issue of financial giving, and are not biblical. We often hear well-meaning Christians disparage giving as only a second-rate form of helping the poor. "I want to do more than just write a check," they say. The implication is that direct ministry to the poor is more valuable than indirect ministry. Where does the Bible establish this kind of merit system? Certainly, Jesus warns that when we give to the poor, we should not attract attention to ourselves (see Matt. 6:2-4); but He does not diminish giving as a form of help for the needy. It's troubling when people create these informal hierarchies that are extra-biblical and act to discourage those who would help in this way. We know that Jesus' ministry team was integrally involved in giving to meet needs, because the night Judas betrayed the Lord, the remaining 11 disciples believed that Judas was headed to give something to the poor.

Clearly, the world needs more people who will live incarnationally among the poor, and for that reason front-line ministry is vital. But that doesn't make it better than the ministries of giving and prayer. In fact, one reason there are not more full-time mission workers among the poor is that there are not enough mission senders. And one reason there are not enough senders is that their peers have hinted that writing checks is copping out.

We live in an interconnected world that offers ever-increasing opportunities of involvement with the poor: working directly on a mission team, helping to send other workers, giving to special needs, and volunteering full- or part-time in specific ministries. All are important; all are necessary.

When God Designs a Society from Scratch

Even more than their harshly treated bodies, the eyes of the poor register the internal scar tissue of people who have suffered for years on the street. The expressions in their eyes vary from desperate scanning to vacant staring to a haunted look that has lost any vestige of light. And there are eyes that appear numb from living private lives in public places. Even so, long after identity has been reduced to a category—a man with leprosy to "leper," a woman who uses to "addict"—the eyes retain uniqueness. Eyes are the fingerprints of the soul.

In the first year of His ministry, Jesus journeyed to Jerusalem and passed through the sheep gate. Near the gate was the pool of Bethesda (House of Mercy), a grand architectural statement with five porticoes and two reflecting pools. The Gospel of John tells us the site was crowded with "a multitude of those who were sick, blind, lame, and withered" (John 5:3). They lay under the columns with the anonymity of bodies that have staked out pavement for years, all waiting to be first into the waters on the rare occasion when an angel of the Lord rippled its surface.

Unfulfilled Expectations

Jesus disregarded the smell of decay and human waste and looked into the eyes of these desperate people. He looked carefully at one man and knew that he had been there for 38 years. How different this scene of misery was from the hopeful images God had outlined to His people centuries before as they journeyed to the Promised Land. Back then God declared, "There should be no poor among you, for in the land the LORD your God is giving you to possess as your inheritance, he will richly bless you" (Deut. 15:4). Same land, same people, same God, but Israel had become one of the poorest regions in the Roman Empire. There were multiple reasons for this, and Jesus was doubtlessly aware of them; still, surveying the scene at Bethesda, He must have felt keen disappointment in His Father's unrealized dreams. Deuteronomy shows us that God took great care to help His people micro-develop an interdependent social system backed by law that would provide for the welfare of all His children. This included sabbatical and jubilee years as well as general admonitions to give generously to the poor "without a grudging heart" (Deut. 15:10).

When I read the passages in the first five books of the Old Testament, outlining the architecture of a just and compassionate society, I get energized. I realize that we have an opportunity today for the people of God to take the lead in this same vision, and that this also creates special opportunities for Christians in the marketplace. I am inspired by the many Christian business people who are working inventively to see that their skills and experience make tangible differences in the lives of poor people here and abroad.

These passages of Scripture and others like them indicate that when God takes a hand in designing our social systems, He wants to ensure the security of the poor, both individually and systemically. For some twenty-first-century Christians wedded to the individualism of modern capitalism, God's "welfare program" feels threatening. The important thing is that God meant for there to be no poor in the land, and we have no reason to believe He has changed His mind today. We often hear people submit Jesus' statement, "the poor you will always have with you" (Matt. 26:11), as evidence that God is somehow resigned to the fact of, or willing to tolerate, poverty. We believe that as the people of God's new covenant, we should be just as concerned today, both individually and systemically, to work toward God's intention of having no poor.

Still, we must not expect that we will ever eliminate poverty. Even during the Exodus journey, God was a realist and anticipated that His people would not always be obedient. "There will always be poor people in the land," He confirmed. "Therefore I command you to be openhanded toward your brothers and toward the poor and needy in your land" (Deut. 15:11). This is a very important verse for twenty-first-century Christians who are motivated primarily by success. Essentially, God clarifies that we will never win the war on poverty. But He goes on to command that we should pursue the battle vigorously. For us this feels like a paradox. Why fight a battle you can't win? But to God, His commands are not contradictory; His economy is indexed to obedience, not performance. We have found this verse to be critical in our spiritual formation as we attempt to wean ourselves from performance and make our incentive biblical obedience.

Jesus Opened His Hand

John records that on His way to the temple, Jesus stopped at
Bethesda to address the need of one invalid man (see John 5:1-14).
He may have helped more people, but it is likely that God called
Jesus to help just the one. It must have been hard for God's Son
to draw Himself away from all those imploring eyes, to know that
on that day, in that place, He did not eliminate all the need. But
Jesus was faithful to open wide His hand, and one man who had
lain for 38 years in the same place not only regained his mobility
but also had the most important encounter of his life.

hinge moments

When you are right, you cannot be too radical;
when you are wrong, you cannot be too conservative.

MARTIN LUTHER KING, JR.

On a hillside above Assisi, in the spring of 1206, a young man full of a passion for God tore off all his clothes and flung them at his father's feet. This young man, whom history has come to call St. Francis, had been dragged before the Bishop of Assisi by his irate father, a wealthy cloth merchant. Francis's father charged Francis with stealing his resources to help the poor and to re-build the crumbling walls of a local chapel.[15]

Frustrated that his motives had been questioned and his best intentions misunderstood, Francis threw everything down on impulse and, perhaps, in a flash of vision. He had glimpsed an unfettered pursuit of Jesus and determined that never again would any barrier beyond the "wall of his own flesh" come between him and the imitation of Christ. Fixing his eyes on his Lord, this son of privilege walked away from the stunned crowd as a beggar.[16] God first gathered around him 12 like-minded young men, and not long thereafter many more. Francis's dramatic break with the world propelled him on a journey that would launch one of the greatest movements to advance the Kingdom in Church history. That day in Assisi, Francis demonstrated that there must be a few in each generation who will shed every vestige of the world, not because it is all bad but because one cannot always be an agent of change and remain inside the system.

Before the break with his father, Francis had taken advantage of his leverage as the son of a well-to-do businessman. As the son and heir, Francis felt entitled to sell some of his father's cloth and distribute the proceeds to charity. In effect, he had been operating within the system. But after his father's attack, Francis determined to break with the world and "follow naked, the naked Christ."[17]

Staking Out New Ground

Would Francis have made the same impact if he had not turned his back on the world and instead remained his father's son, an apprentice cloth merchant who acted benevolently on the side?

That day when Francis was hauled before the bishop, he did more than stand his ground with his father; he staked out new ground. Francis pushed beyond the limits of charity in the established order of things to found a new kind of missionary order, one set apart from a church struggling with corruption and one less likely to be compromised. Francis interpreted Scripture literally and concretely. When Jesus admonished His disciples to go out with no bag, no purse, no shoes, Francis and his followers did likewise. And unlike orders founded before his time, Francis's convictions to live like the early apostles included commitments both to simple living and to evangelism.

Ultimately, the new ground Francis and his brothers in Christ discovered gave rise to a long tradition of pioneering ministry among the poor. In the early years, they grew exponentially and also inspired the emergence of a remarkable order of nuns called the Poor Clares. The movement we call the Franciscans today was first called the Order of Friars Minor. These men not only offered a radical pursuit of holiness but also nurtured a contemplative spirituality that encouraged encounter with Jesus among the poor in a way that was transforming for the missionary and the receiving community alike.[18]

Francis was cutting-edge. In the late twentieth century, the term "cutting-edge" gained great currency. Every organization, every entrepreneur wanted to be cutting-edge—so did churches and mission organizations. In reality, only a few were. Most tried to be cutting-edge from within the middle of the pack. One insightful observation of the twentieth-century Western Church comes from Vincent Harding's poem "Light in the Asphalt Jungle": "They tried to save and be safe at the same time" (to innovate yet eliminate risk).

Francis did not try to be safe. Nor did he try to be cutting-edge. His authentic pursuit of God simply took him to the creative margins. Francis's faith was so radical that it sparked renewal in both church and society until the Reformation 300 years later.[19]

Ministry From the Margins

Was Francis's impact an anomaly, or does God renew His people in upside-down ways, from the margins?

In his first letter to the church in Corinth, Paul wrote, "But God chose the foolish things of the world to shame the wise; God chose the weak things of the world to shame the strong. He chose the lowly things of this world and the despised things—and the things that are not—to nullify the things that are, so that no one may boast before him" (1 Cor. 1:27-29).

That God works radical change through humble, unlikely means is echoed throughout Scripture and Church history. Jericho was conquered partly through the efforts of the prostitute Rahab. Nehemiah took a remnant of exiles back to Jerusalem in the teeth of their enemies to rebuild the city walls. Gideon's army of 300 is one of the most striking examples. God was not content to war against Midian with conventional arms and strength in numbers. He pared Gideon's force to 300 and directed them against their enemies with trumpets and empty pitchers. God explained to Gideon, "The [troops] who are with you are too many for Me to give Midian into their hands, for Israel would become boastful, saying, 'My own power has delivered me'" (Judg. 7:2, *NASB*).

Early in his ministry, John Wesley came to a similar conclusion. In his journal, dated May 21, 1764, he observed: "I preached at Haddington . . . to a very elegant congregation. But I expect little good will be done here, for we begin at the wrong end;

religion must not go from the greatest to the least or the power would appear to be of men."[20]

The dynamic story of King David gives a glimpse of God fashioning a sidelined minority into an effective, alternative community. Midway through King Saul's reign, God grew dissatisfied with Saul's wayward leadership. He set about raising David the shepherd boy, last and least of an ordinary family in the smallest tribe of Israel. God gathered people around David from the margins, and they formed an alternative community to Saul's status quo. "All those who were in distress or in debt or discontented gathered around him, and he became their leader. About four hundred men were with him" (1 Sam. 22:2). Four hundred against Saul's trained thousands is not exactly a critical mass. David and his ragged army, fleeing from cave to cave, barely a step ahead of the government, must have looked like a rabble. But seen with the eyes of faith, they were mighty men.

Probably, at first, they didn't feel like mighty men. For years, they were simply David's followers. But with time and the chemistry of gifted leadership, commitment and experience, these battle-hardened few became a formidable force.

Scripture records several images of David's men. First, we see them as the rag-tag "in debt" and "discontented." About midway in the process, their numbers and experience having grown steadily, they are camped at Ziklag where the writer of Chronicles describes their skill and valor and gives us an impressive list of men (see 1 Chron. 12:1-22). A final glimpse shows that David's entire army (see 2 Sam. 10:7), likely numbered in the tens of thousands, came to be called by that same name as the original few: "the mighty men." That is the power of modeling. David's original supporting cast set a standard of valor and integrity that the rest of the army ultimately lived up to.

But this was years later. In the beginning, they were only a few malcontents and misfits. Where were the well adjusted? Where was the mainstream? Where were the people of Israel—God's chosen?

They were with Saul.

Those who seek to go among the poor today and go against the grain of contemporary culture must seek also to understand the nature of the mainstream. Israel, at least the bulk of them, was following Saul in a direction that God had abandoned. "Now the Spirit of the LORD had departed from Saul" (1 Sam. 16:14).

How can the majority of God's people have been so blind to the absence of God's Spirit—so grounded in groupthink? Why did they not rally to David until well after he was a safe bet? It wasn't until after Saul's death that all the people joined David.

At Hebron, the people proclaimed David king and, amazingly, told him that they knew he had been God's choice all along: "All the tribes of Israel came to David at Hebron and said, 'We are your own flesh and blood. In the past, while Saul was king over us, you were the one who led Israel on their military campaigns. And the LORD said to you, "You will shepherd my people Israel, and you will become their ruler"'" (2 Sam. 5:1-2).

Not Going with the Flow

It was not so easy to leave the status quo, even after the truth had left it. After all, Saul still had the power, and in him was order and security.

David's journey reveals again a God who delights in working His most radical change through a fringe, a remnant. Small numbers are not necessarily a sign that God is indifferent or that the direction is wrong or lacks legitimacy. Quite the opposite may be true. God was actively present in the lives of both Francis of Assisi and David when the following for each man was so small in number as to appear inconsequential.

It is not easy to look back hundreds of years and fully appreciate how counterintuitive it is to proceed faithfully in a new direction with such little support. The wisdom of hindsight reveals that God's Spirit was with the remnant who were following Francis and David. It is another thing altogether to forge

No Human Involved
John Hayes

In 1990, Dave Everitt, one of our InnerCHANGE members living on Minnie Street, heard a commotion in his back parking lot. He went out to find a crowd rapidly gathering around two police officers. Off to the side, about 50 feet away, four men stood, appearing quite agitated.

As Dave drew closer, he saw that the police were standing over a man in the last stages of the death struggle. Because his central nervous system had not yet shut down, his arms and legs continued to twitch, despite the fact that he was already dead.

Dave asked the neighborhood kids what had happened. One said that the man had been caught breaking into a car. The kids pointed to the four men standing uneasily on the

ahead with a tiny band in the present, directly into the headwinds of cultural inertia.

Nearly 1 in 10 verses in the Bible speaks of the poor in some way. Ronald Rolheiser points out that it is inarguable that the poor are central to God's heart.[21] In a perfect world there should "be no one in need among you" (Deut. 15:4). In our fallen world, we are called to open our hearts and hands to those in need. Yet, in the West, the majority of Christians with financial resources do not work among the poor and many do not even have a meaningful relationship with anyone who is poor.

The mainstream, by definition, goes with the flow, not against it. The history of God's people attests to this. The writer

sidelines and described how those four had caught the man stealing the car, broken his legs with baseball bats so that he couldn't run, stabbed him in the back and, finally, clubbed him on the head until he was dead.

Dave stood there, in horror and awe, wondering what to say about a man who lives and dies suddenly, senselessly—alone? What can you say about a man who risks his life and loses it forever for something so small as a car?

As far as the police were concerned, the incident was an NHI: No Human Involved. NHI is a label police use among themselves to refer to homicides in the seamy side of the city where neither suspects nor witnesses can be easily identified and where no one steps forward on behalf of the victim.

In other words, NHI describes murders no one cares about.

Despite the fact that the killers were there, and witnesses were there, the police informally but effectively pronounced the incident "No Human Involved." As far as any of us ever knew,

of Hebrews, speaking of Jesus who "suffered outside the city gate," urged believers to "go to him outside the camp, bearing the disgrace he bore" (Heb. 13:12-13). In order to live the gospel among the poor, we must expect to go outside the gate and break away from the system. And we should expect to discover Christ there and follow His lead, especially when we are acting against injustice. Most people applaud and admire works of mercy. When it comes to speaking against systemic injustice in a way that might entail changing life-styles or sharing power and influence, however, there comes an awkward silence.

there was no investigation, no arrest, no trial. NHI may well have been the last word on that man's life.

Later, I thought, *No Human Involved was probably the most fitting epitaph for the murdered man.* He had lived and died invisibly. But the phrase also aptly sums up the lives of poor people all over the world. Very few poor live anything like front-page lives. More often than not, the poor remain faceless and voiceless.

The poor may not make news, but they do make history. As we have found in sub-merging, God is chronicling their contribution for those with eyes to see. ✳

A Call to Order

Those who choose to live and work among the poor should expect to serve Christ as a remnant. You can hope for more to join in, certainly. Celebrate those who come. But do not wait for a critical mass from the mainstream to act. Be content to work far from the limelight. And don't expect the mainstream to validate or embrace your efforts among the poor with your same intensity or passion.

Living and ministering among the poor can be complex and rigorous and is rarely effective as a solo affair. Like the early Franciscans, the Poor Clares and David's mighty men, God must be allowed to build communities where the whole is greater than

Minnie Street

the sum of its parts. This kind of synergy can be gained only when team formation is a priority. Too often mission expeditions use geography alone to gather teams rather than use complementary fitness among the individuals that expresses the fullness of the Body of Christ.

However, there are also dangers in being the committed few. A cynicism toward the mainstream can easily creep in. We must remind ourselves that Saul's mainstream eventually became David's main body, and he integrated them with grace. Small communities can breed spiritual smugness. Pharisaism is a disease the committed can fall prey to—so one must guard against becoming self-congratulatory.

The World of Francis

In his excellent work *The Friars: The Impact of the Early Mendicant Movement on Western Society,* C. H. Lawrence describes the sociopolitical dimension of Francis's world and maintains that the Franciscan order was a revolutionary solution to a potentially explosive situation. Lawrence describes the thirteenth-century Church as an institution in crisis with no appropriate response to the "newly arisen urban and secular culture." The emergence of this potent, secular culture in the cities came about through "medieval Europe's economic miracle"—more than two centuries of dynamic economic and demographic expansion beginning in the eleventh century.[22] Lawrence notes nine qualities that helped to create the hunger during this period for a fresh movement, such as the rise of the Franciscans:

1. A sustained rise in population that accelerated urbanization, pushing growth past city walls into new "suburbs."
2. An accelerated growth of international trade, tying world economies into some unhealthy dependency relationships.
3. A tendency for cities to dominate the political scene, and new urban values to overshadow traditional rural ones.
4. A breakdown of traditional community ties, promoting feelings of isolation and spiritual drift.
5. Inability of the traditional church, rooted in rural strategies, to respond to urban needs, and the rise of cults and heresies to fill the void.
6. A tendency for economies to become more and more market-driven, pursuing profit as the only bottom line.
7. The widening of the gap between rich and poor.
8. The rise of an urban middle and upper-middle class who were increasingly literate and increasingly dissatisfied with the church's monopoly on learning.
9. A rise in literacy, the rediscovery of Aristotle and the classics, the founding of secular universities, bringing about Europe's entry into an "age of information," and the concept of knowledge, not only resources or inherited title, as a source of power.[23]

With a virtual monopoly on all things religious, without the Protestant Reformation and the emergence of Christian denominations to usher in freshness and bring in checks and balances, the arteries of the Church had begun to harden. Church leaders were still using only Latin in an increasingly pluralistic Europe that was fast leaving Latin behind.[24]

Heavy with riches acquired over centuries and slowed by a spirituality weighed down by allegory, the world of Francis hungered for spiritual models that were concrete, relevant and light-footed. Ordinary people sought a more literal interpretation for Jesus' call to "Follow me!" rather than simply a puzzlement over Christ's "deeper meaning." Amid the Church's increasingly self-indulgent complexity, there was a tremendous yearning among lay people for the golden age of the apostles.[25]

Of course, the human heart's longing for a way of life and faith that is pure, practical and free of greed also has a potential dark side to it. Both sides of this longing, light and dark, are exploited indirectly by mass media messages, an increasing value

Hinge Moment Missed
John Hayes

In 1490, two years before Christopher Columbus made his historic voyage to the Americas, Portuguese missionaries established a mission to the Congo. Only eight years before, explorers had found the mouth of the Congo River, and as was the custom in Europe, efforts to evangelize the local people followed quickly in the wake of national and commercial interests. It is difficult now to get a feel for how well supported this Christian effort to evangelize may have been—records are scant. What we do know is that there was much conversion among the tribes in the last decade of the fifteenth century. The king and queen of Congo became converts and took the names John and Eleonora. Their oldest son followed suit, took the name Affonso, and was baptized in 1491. His vision was to see tribes in the Congo

placed on speed, and in a more direct way, by countless cults and despots the world over. In Cambodia during the 1970s, for example, the Khmer Rouge tried to turn the clock back to "Year Zero," its golden age of rural empire.

Business Unusual

St. Francis stepped into a world swinging on a hinge. Around him, God gathered passionately committed young men and women to form the Order of Friars Minor and the Poor Clares, alternative communities that could model faith to a desperate, unsettled world. Could we be in a similar hinge moment in our

become Christian and comprise the first Christian kingdom in what was then called "tropical" Africa.

He had trouble getting the Portuguese religious authorities to take his yearning seriously. The expatriate missionaries left, one by one, or died, and the Portuguese Church did not replace them. Don Affonso then sent a number of young men of good standing, including his eldest son, Don Henrique, to Lisbon to be mentored in the faith. He hoped they would come back to indigenize the Church in Congo.

Religious leaders in Lisbon had no vision to mentor these young men, however. As a result, Don Henrique did not return to the Congo for 20 years. When he finally returned in 1521, he died of disease soon after. Heartbroken, Don Affonso proceeded to establish an indigenous seminary, though leaders in Lisbon counseled against it. He even went against the grain of African culture of the time and founded Christian schools for girls. For a time, the young church flourished, but the few Portuguese observers left in

own history? In a world with so much up in the air, might God want to ground faith and commitment once again in practical, passionate ways through new, relevant, sacramental orders?

In InnerCHANGE, more than a decade ago, this is indeed what we began to feel. We sensed an impulse from God to create highly dedicated mission orders and communities among the poor, an activity that Scott Bessenecker beautifully describes in his book *The New Friars* as "God's recurring dream."[27]

We have been joined by another mission order among the poor, Urban Neighbors of Hope, an Australian-based order we had the privilege of mentoring in its early years. Other orders and communities with a focus on justice are currently emerg-

---

Congo believed that a lack of mentoring from mature believers allowed the church to slip into cultural abuses, notably authoritarianism. Soon after Don Affonso's death, the Christian Church in Congo withered. By 1650, it is said there was no longer a trace of the vision to see Congo established as a Christian kingdom.

Five centuries ago, Portuguese church leaders failed to see and share a vision for an authentic indigenous church in the Congo, failing also to recognize their critical role in serving as midwife to the process. One historian summarized the missed opportunity: "The Portuguese were more concerned for commerce than Christianity, and Don Affonso died disillusioned."[26] ✳

ing in Europe and the United States.

We live in an exciting time, full of possibility, but one that is sobering as well. Even as advances are made against wretched need in parts of the world, poverty deepens in others. Old segregations based on race are reconfirmed, and new segregations are created behind the razor wire of class—divisions that limit the access of whole peoples to the good news of the kingdom of God. Bono, leader of the internationally renowned rock group U2, writes compellingly of the hinge moment we find ourselves in:

> We could be the first generation to outlaw the kind of extreme, stupid poverty that sees a child die of hunger

InnerCHANGE, Minneapolis

in a world of plenty, or of a disease preventable by a twenty-cent innoculation. . . . We can't say our generation couldn't afford to do it. And we can't say our generation didn't have reason to do it. It's up to us. We can choose to shift the responsibility, or we can choose to shift the paradigm.[28]

submerging

*The Word
became flesh
with hands
to draw in dirt
clearing away the
stained bed sheets
stirring hearts
homeless
visiting the paralytic
through friends.*

—LAILA BLANCHARD

In the last years of the first century, the last apostle left alive was nearing the end of his life. In his final thoughts, he turned to the beginning: "That which was from the beginning, which we have heard, which we have seen with our eyes, which we have looked at and our hands have touched" (1 John 1:1). The apostle John

The Cost of Commitment
Ashley Barker

In the late nineteenth century, Father Damien, a Belgian priest from the Order of the Sacred Heart, sensed a call to go to the poor. He ended up living and serving among the sick in an isolated Hawaiian leper colony. At first, Father Damien would visit the colony, which was blocked off from the rest of society by a huge cliff face. He would arrive by boat, go from house to house providing food and medicines, and then go back to the broader society. This was a huge risk, as Hawaiians thought leprosy to be so contagious and dangerous that it might wipe out their society altogether.

Yet Father Damien did not stop at service provision. He eventually made his home in the leper colony and was soon banned from wider society along with those he served. One day in the chapel he helped build, he began his sermon with the now-famous phrase "We lepers . . ." Not long after this, he caught leprosy himself. Rather than go back to Europe where he could have treatment, he stayed because, as he said, "None of the other lepers had that choice." Father Damien died on that island, far from his native Belgium, of a leprosy-related disease.[29]

The mystery and the inspiration of the incarnation is that the Word became flesh and blood and moved into the neighborhood.

It is easy to grow impatient in ministry. Often we don't see enough transformation. Father Damien's example reminds us that real compassion means suffering alongside. Pity weeps and walks away, so the saying goes. Compassion comes to help and stay. ✳

was recalling his life as the disciple John and those dynamic early years when he and 11 others experienced the presence of Jesus in a way they could see, hear and touch. The phrase "our hands have touched" leaves no doubt that they followed someone who was accessible, personal, even vulnerable. John was drawing a portrait of Christ as much more than an engaging speaker who could press the flesh in the crowd. The apostle was describing a companion on the road for three extraordinary years, the intimate master of the upper room who was content to let John recline against Him in the last and most painful supper of His life.

John's record of Jesus' tangible, tactile incarnation is compelling. He wrote these words to a church in crisis, a church that needed to be reminded that Jesus came to Earth in a human body. This was not just hearsay. This was not a dream, a vision, or a rare, circulating manuscript. Today, as in every generation, the world needs Christians who allow themselves to be not only seen and heard, but also touched. Many, like the disciple Thomas, will come groping in the dark toward a truth they can read from our living bodies, like Braille.

We live in an age of information, of mass messages. It is an era with an uncanny ability to multiply words. Yet an increasing number of the world's people live lives without real change and without Christ. The world doesn't need more words, not even more "right" words. *The world needs more words made flesh.* The world needs more people to live the good news incarnationally, in a way that can be seen, heard and handled.

InnerCHANGE workers have been handled—often roughly! Work among the poor steers you into a lot of heavy emotional traffic. Those of us who live in poor communities have been threatened, knocked down and even shaken down by confused police. We have seen our cars vandalized, homes robbed and have been held up at gunpoint. Some have encountered sexual advances, stumbled into gun battles, and stopped gang fights. We have been exposed to and suffered serious diseases that go with close living and poor hygiene. Compelled, like Ezekiel, to be ones who would stand in the gap on behalf of poor communities, some of us have found ourselves repeatedly standing in the crossfire.

Most of the time, though, we have been handled with love. Our experiences among the poor have yielded some of the most poignant moments of our lives, some of the most humorous and most deeply satisfying. And in the handling, we've discovered our own need to handle—to push out the boundaries of our intimacy and encounter our deepest selves.

Four Dimensions of Incarnational Ministry

To persevere in our callings and experience some of the most profound adventures of our lives, it helps to understand the great strength of the incarnational model of ministry and its various dimensions. Incarnational ministry among the poor works powerfully on four levels—as *a model, a method, a message* and *a spiritual discipline*. We have found that when teams begin with only a vague idea of what it means to minister as poor among the poor, they frequently end up disillusioned.

1) The *Model* of Christ

In perhaps the supreme statement of the Incarnation, John declared, "The Word became flesh and made his dwelling among us" (John 1:14). John added that believers are sent out in the same way that Jesus was sent (17:18).

The apostle Paul wrote, "Your attitude should be the same as that of Christ Jesus: Who, being in very nature God, did not consider equality with God something to be grasped, but made himself nothing, taking the very nature of a servant, being made in human likeness" (Phil. 2:5-7). Again, in a letter to the Corinthians, Paul wrote, "For you know the grace of our Lord Jesus Christ, that though He was rich, yet for your sake He became poor, so that you through His poverty might become rich" (2 Cor. 8:9, *NASB*).

Taking Christ's example seriously has been the first step for generations of disciples to recover the fresh power of the Early Church. Inspired by a vision of the apostolic life, it became a matter of principle for Francis of Assisi and other pioneers of reform to renounce worldly possessions and "follow naked the naked Christ."[30] In fact, my research indicates that nearly every reform or period of revitalization in Church history is marked at least in part by a profound conviction to simplify lifestyle.

Incarnational ministry has been a provocative subject throughout the centuries as Christians have disagreed over its definition and application. Upon arriving in Japan for her first tour of duty, missionary Amy Carmichael was reprimanded for "going native." She believed she was just living simply and appropriately in the culture and lamented that her peers had settled for so anemic a Christianity. "I don't wonder that apostolic miracles have died," she wrote in her journal. "Apostolic living certainly has."

Like St. Francis and many others whose faith inspires imitation, we choose to live simply among the poor not just because it helps bind us to them, but also because it helps bind us to our Savior and His kingdom.

2) The *Method* of Incarnational Ministry

Incarnational ministry, one soon discovers, is a very practical way of reaching poor neighbors. One must always earn the right to be heard, and insiders are better than outsiders in communicating good news among a host culture. Living with and like the poor hastens language and culture learning, helps demonstrate that we are for real, and places us near the heartbeat of poor communities.

The apostle Paul described the method of incarnational ministry when he wrote:

> To the Jews I became like a Jew, to win the Jews. To those under the law I became like one under the law (though I myself am not under the law), so as to win those under the law. To those not having the law I became like one not having the law (though I am not free from God's law but am under Christ's law), so as to win those not having the law. To the weak I became weak, to win the weak. I have become all things to all men so that by all possible means I might save some. I do all this for the sake of the gospel, that I may share in its blessings (1 Cor. 9:20-23).

3) The *Message* of Incarnational Ministry

The apostle Paul wrote to the Romans that God "did not spare his own Son, but gave him up for us all" (Rom. 8:32). Incarnational ministry recognizes that love is real and that it can be costly.

When we move into a poor neighborhood, we send the message that if love is costly, then those who are the object of such love are worth much. This is especially important to the poor who bear the weight of the world's low opinion of them. G. K. Chesterton wrote, "No plans or proposals or efficient rearrangements will give back to a broken man his self respect and sense of speaking with an equal. [But] one gesture will do it."[31]

In choosing to move into communities of poor people and live with them, however, we send more than a message of love that helps raise low self-esteem. We validate hope by showing our neighbors that we entrust ourselves to the same upside-down gospel that we proclaim. In living with the poor, we express with our lives that we believe God when He declares that those of "humble circumstances" may "glory in [their] high position" (Jas. 1:9, *NASB*), and that in His economy, the poor are raised to "sit with nobles and inherit a seat of honor" (1 Sam. 2:8, *NASB*).

Equally important, when we move into neighborhoods in which indigenous Christians are already present, we position ourselves to serve them and learn from them and help dissolve the illusion that we are outside experts. We cannot emphasize enough the importance of appreciating and working with those whom God has already placed in the neighborhood. Though InnerCHANGE workers typically have sensed calls to neighborhoods with few Christians present, we have seen how disempowering it can be for local Christians when missionaries move into their midst, anxious to pursue primarily their own agenda.

How does disempowerment come about? First, when we do not relocate among the poor, we risk sending a message that their environments are too toxic for "good" Christians to live in.

This adds to their emotional scar tissue and can lead the poor to conclude that the state of their income is of graver significance than the state of their souls. Second, in neighborhoods in which indigenous Christians are already present, commuter ministries that can out-resource local efforts can be very divisive. We have seen this quiet conflict develop, time and again, when large, wealthy churches commute to minister in poor neighborhoods, usually with children and youth. Indigenous Christian parents will rarely complain publicly, but ultimately, this approach can disempower them.

Finally, incarnational ministry acts as a message of love and grace to the mission workers themselves that it is okay to be human. In living among the poor, we cannot help but lower the bullet-proof shield that separates the professional service provider from the poor. Consequently, we open ourselves to good news *from* the poor.

No other communities are as observant as poor communities. Unlike the suburbs, where people often are insulated by a 60-plus-hour work week, high fences and alarm systems, people in poor communities usually know their neighbors. They hang out. They see one another. And what they don't see, they hear through paper-thin walls. So it is impossible for the Christian worker to maintain a facade for long—impossible to quick-change from Clark Kent to Superman to gratify our spiritual egos every time we go out the door to "do ministry." The fish-bowl environment of most poor communities levels the ground between Christian workers and those they serve to such a degree that often the hurts in the "healer" can be revealed and made whole in the process of ministry. This vulnerability allows people to see that we are human, and then our Christianity appears to them less remote, more accessible, more credible.

4) Incarnational Ministry as *Spiritual Discipline*

For centuries, believers have committed themselves to poverty for seasons or even for their whole lives as a means of spiritual gain. Jesus' admonition to the rich young ruler—"If you want to be perfect, go, sell your possessions and give to the poor, and you will have treasure in heaven. Then come, follow me" (Matt. 19:21)—is a passage often cited as encouragement to live a life of material loss for spiritual gain. But in some ways, Christ's commissioning of the 70 in Luke is more appropriate: "Go! I am sending you out like lambs among wolves. Do not take a purse or bag or sandals; and do not greet anyone on the road" (Luke 10:3). Here the impulse to strip one's life is less for spiritual perfection than to kindle dependence upon God as a foundation to the missionary journey. In both of these examples, living simply among the poor acts as a spiritual discipline. It helps wean us away from self-reliance to God-reliance.

Moving in geographically to embrace the poor and share our lives with them introduces a second spiritual discipline: doing justice and sharing mercy among the poor. This is both a compassionate and a devotional act. As Isaiah described this discipline, it is a form of spiritual fasting.

> Is not this the kind of fasting that I have chosen: to loose the chains of injustice and untie the cords of the yoke, to set the oppressed free and break every yoke? Is

it not to share your food with the hungry and to provide the poor wanderer with shelter—when you see the naked, to clothe him, and not to turn away from your own flesh and blood? (Isa. 58:6–7).

Sharing our lives with the poor serves as a spiritual fast—a discipline for our personal growth, not as a way of renouncing the world in arid asceticism but as a way of joining with Jesus to embrace the world's feet and wash them.

A Creative Tension

The above four dimensions operate in creative tension. As *model*, incarnational ministry provides a kind of spiritual leverage in that it places the mission worker in the footsteps of Jesus as "God with us."

As *method*, incarnational ministry provides relational leverage that helps us become cultural insiders and humble learners.

As *message*, incarnational ministry offers inspirational leverage in that it recalls a higher vision of God's love for the world in restoring dignity to the poor.

Finally, as *spiritual discipline*, incarnational ministry among the poor enhances the Christian's personal growth by cultivating godly dependence and dethroning consumerism, which distracts from intimacy with God.

When we lose sight of these four dimensions operating together, we fail to experience the synergy that confirms the whole as greater than the sum of its parts. And we can end up creating disadvantages rather than advantages of incarnational ministry.

For example, thinking that incarnational ministry is *the* model can lead to unpleasant self-righteousness and dogmatism that insists incarnational ministry is the best or only way.

Overemphasis on the method of incarnational ministry can engender attitudes of utilitarianism and a dry professionalism.

Employed excessively or exclusively as a message, incarnational ministry makes mission staff and volunteers vulnerable to developing a messiah complex, an over-identification with ourselves as Christ. Western Christians must especially beware of falling prey to this sense of self-importance in the two-thirds world in which the effects of colonialism are still very much alive.

Without appreciating these three dimensions, the incarnational approach becomes little more than careful contextualization, an exercise in social science to be pursued only to the extent that it works.

Finally, a preoccupation with incarnational ministry as spiritual discipline can bring about self-absorption and false humility, and can ultimately steer us away from the essential selflessness of mission. When we choose this path, we voluntarily choose to live among and with the poor. We must remember that poverty as a means of spiritual perfection holds little or no appeal to those for whom there is no exit clause.

Our experience has shown us that to undervalue one or more of the four dimensions of incarnational ministry threatens sustainability, pressures team life needlessly and risks the stability of long-term relationships and accomplishments.

Incarnational Ministry as a Process

These four dimensions are all integral parts of the process of incarnational ministry, a process that requires balance, strength and attention to detail.

Moving the process too quickly endangers long-term mission sustainability and creates unrealistic expectations within the host community. Journeying at a patient pace can be hard for Western Christian workers in this frenzied age in which we are conditioned to seize life, get the series of punch lines, and skip the story. Incarnational ministry is a careful, negotiated process—a courtship that includes the Christian worker, the

Life Support
John Hayes

Deanna and I were packing to go to Los Angeles for a leadership meeting, and then I would head to Wheaton, Illinois, to speak and recruit at a conference. I would be out of town for two weeks. The last thing I wanted to do was answer the phone when it rang. It was one of our neighbors from the Valencia Gardens housing project, telephoning from San Francisco General Hospital to report that a 17-year-old was there on life support. This young man, whom I will call Derrick, was the only son of one of our good friends at Valencia Gardens. We had been living next to Valencia Gardens for only a few months, but we had quickly formed close relationships with families there, and Derrick's family was one of them. There was no question in our minds. We must drive over to give support

host culture and team members in the mission work group and in the host community, all guided by the Holy Spirit.

When Christian workers first arrive in a poor community, they cannot yet know what meaningful sacrifices they will make in terms of comfort and income. These kinds of insights are best gathered as the mission worker looks to those who have gone before and, even more important, takes on mentors in the host community who can impart what it means to grow up in the culture and economy of that particular community.

To parachute into a community with a preconceived idea of what constitutes a simple lifestyle not only assumes that we have already stripped ourselves of the worst aspects of our

to his family and pray for him.

Several months earlier, Derrick was stabbed in the face during an altercation. At first the wound did not seem serious, but soon it became apparent that the knife had made an opening to the brain, exposing it to serious infection. Derrick had to go to the hospital every day for a month to get antibiotic injections.

Derrick seemed to improve. He was a big, strong guy. The summer before, he had been shot in the leg, drove himself to the hospital and returned the next day with a cane. So, although everyone took his new injury seriously, no one was overly worried. But early that morning, when we were packing, Derrick awoke with a severe headache, and his mother drove him to the hospital. Within a few hours, Derrick lost consciousness, experienced a series of seizures and fell into a coma. Just before losing consciousness, Derrick called out to his mother. She rushed to tell him it would be all right but was never able to speak to him again.

own culture but also presumes that we already know what the Kingdom looks like in that new setting. This attitude denies our hosts the opportunity to become a part of our pilgrimage and denies them the opportunity to teach us what we need to learn from them.

Jesus did not turn up in Nazareth at the age of 30. He began in the womb, grew up as a Jew, subjected Himself to His parents and seated Himself at the feet of the elders. He lived and moved and had His being in a specific community and culture, and learned from that community and culture.

Moses, however, gives us a biblical example of one who moved too quickly and naively into his ministry among the poor

When we arrived at the hospital, the waiting room was full with family and neighbors. I was heartened to see Helen among them, the mom of my favorite six-year-old, Maurice. Maurice's dad had been shot and killed three years earlier, so I had taken him under my wing. In tears, Derrick's mother rushed over to hug us. I was touched to see her give attention to Savannah, our two-year-old. We discovered that Derrick had slipped into a coma because he had developed meningitis as a consequence of the face wound. Because the nurses were concerned that Derrick was contagious, Deanna and I decided that I would go into the room to pray and she would stay in the waiting room to give comfort.

Helen led me down the hall to the ICU. I began to generate the determination to pray in faith for this young man I barely knew, so I only half-listened to Helen telling me that Maurice had just gotten his report card and that he had wanted to come over immediately to show me. I walked into the

before he had all the learning experiences he needed.

Eyes That Look

Moses grew up with advantages that made him particularly well suited to be an agent of change among the oppressed Hebrews. Pharaoh's daughter gave him a royal upbringing in the palace, and his Hebrew mother instilled in him a faith in God and sensitivity to injustice. He began life cradled in a basket for protection and grew up cradled in a palace for privilege. His Egyptian name, Moses ("Because I drew him out of the water"), gave him a sense of destiny as a rescued one, and perhaps inclined him to act as a rescuer. Moses was powerful: he was networked, bilingual,

room where Derrick lay on life support in stillness more final than sleep. Two of his friends were keeping silent vigil in the corner. There was the sound of the ventilator, the glow of multiple dials and, in the outside corridors, the squeak of padded shoes.

Praying for healing is one of the aspects of the Christian life about which I have the broadest range of emotions. On the one hand, I have seen God heal dramatically over the years. On the other hand, more often than not, I have seen God not intervene instantaneously. In the case of Derrick, already dead but for the life support, I knew this was a "rise from the dead and walk" situation, if his body were to be healed.

The faith with which I approached Derrick was not industrial strength. It was a mix of faith and fear. I was hopeful that God would intervene and return Derrick to his mother in the way He had done 2,000 years before with another only Son. For a while I prayed quietly—more listening than interceding. Then I prayed aloud, asking God to restore the young man's life.

well educated and accustomed to leadership.

Moses may have been top-heavy with expectations, however: the expectations of two mothers, two households, two cultures, two languages. He carried those expectations with only half the normal identity security, because these two cultures inside him were locked outside of him in a conflicted, master/slave relationship. Moses at 40 was at an age that we in the twenty-first century associate with midlife turning points (see Acts 7:23), as well as midlife "crises."

Exodus 2:11-12 describes how this unique man of God made a life turn and became a man with a mission. "One day, after Moses had grown up, he went out to where his own people were

I lingered for a bit at the bedside, and then moved heavily toward the door.

Outside the room, Helen was waiting for me and read my disappointment. She started again to encourage me with news of Maurice and my effect on him. I appreciated her concern for me but gave her words about as much attention as I would give background music at the dentist's office. When she saw how preoccupied I was, she came around to stand in front of me, pointed back in the direction of Derrick's room and said, "John, that is the reason we're glad you came to Valencia Gardens! We don't want our sons to end up like that anymore. In 10 years, I don't want it to be Maurice you have to go in and pray for like that."

I waited until I was outside before I cried. ✳

and watched them at their hard labor. He saw an Egyptian beating a Hebrew, one of his own people. Glancing this way and that and seeing no one, he killed the Egyptian and hid him in the sand."

Twice in verse 11, we're shown that Moses made a critical life choice. He identified the Jews, not the Egyptians, as "his" people and determined to intercede for them. But Moses made the mistake that many young missionaries make in choosing a people and seeking to reach out to and intercede for them.

In his heart Moses decided that he was a Jew, but does verse 11 say that the Jews respond by taking him in as a Jew? Who are his people? Moses is bilingual, but is he truly bicultural? Had he taken the time to "incarnate" among the Hebrews? Had he

John with Maurice

made key relationships? Had he changed his address to live among them? Had he listened to their painful stories? Did he understand something of the psychology of being on the bottom? All we are told is that Moses looked on their hard labors. But had he really *seen*?

J. Oswald Sanders wrote, "Eyes that look are common; eyes that see are rare." If we are truly to incarnate among the poor, we must go beyond looking at conditions to really seeing as God wants us to see. That type of seeing includes recognizing how the host community *sees us*. Incarnating as a careful process means taking time to court a community and allowing God to set us up to be received by them.

After deliberating for 40 years, Moses rushed suddenly into ministry, acted unwisely and paid for it. The day after he killed the Egyptian, he tried to settle a fight between Jews and was shouted at: "Who made you ruler and judge over us? Are you thinking of killing me as you killed the Egyptian?" (Exod. 2:14). He was sidelined another 40 years in the desert before God called him again into service for the needy and oppressed Hebrews. Acts 7:25 summarizes Moses' first steps in his ministry career: "Moses thought that his own people would realize that God was using him to rescue them, but they did not."

Grace Space

Moses found that idealism was not enough; indeed, idealism can cloud vision. The story of his first act of ministry on behalf of the oppressed is crucial for us as mission workers if we have been accustomed to privilege and to leading. On the other hand, if we conclude from Moses' story that middle- and upper-class Christians from dominant cultures have no legitimacy among the poor, then we conclude too superficially. Moses was recalled, and every bit of his unique background was necessary to allow God to deliver His people and lead them to the land of promise. Exodus 2 expresses important messages to two communities that we should not overlook. Moses' independent action was well intentioned but misguided and reveals how tempting it is for those of us brought up in privileged circumstances to act impulsively on our own. Like Moses, we may enter into poor communities acting authentically from a genuine desire to help. But like Moses, we typically neglect to see how the host community sees us. Moses did not fully realize how much he walked, talked and behaved like an Egyptian. This lack of self-awareness was confirmed later when Moses (again the rescuer) defended the daughters of the priest of Midian. When the daughters returned to their father, they said, "An Egyptian rescued us from the shepherds" (Exod. 2:19).

On the other hand, Exodus 2 reveals how difficult it is for oppressed communities to empower from within. The Bible tells us that the Hebrew people struggled under Egyptian slavery for 400 years. Yet in that time, no Hebrew leader emerged from within to deliver the people. Exodus 2:13-14 vividly shows how disabling oppressive poverty can be. Here, two Hebrew men were fighting with each other instead of expressing solidarity in the face of Egyptian oppression. Furthermore, these same two men could not look past Moses' clumsy first missional act to recognize the help he was offering at the potential cost of his own life. Forty years later, we see again how years of being at the bottom of the social and economic structure can diminish a culture's capacity for hope. Moses declared that God heard the groans of the Hebrews and that He would deliver them from Egypt and carry them into a promised land. Exodus 6:9 reports, "But they did not listen to him because of their discouragement and cruel bondage."

The Exodus story gives us insight into why God continues to call missionaries to cross cultures often at great expense. The Hebrews' behavior shows us how it is possible to get mired in a rut of cultural narrow-mindedness. Moses actually experiences the brunt of cultural tunnel vision from both cultures that represent his heritage. Bob Ekblad, director of a ministry to marginalized migrant workers in the state of Washington, maintains that the Exodus message is good news to the Egyptian empire, not only to the Hebrews. Acting as slave overlords disfigures the Egyptians as children of God made in His image.[32] But when Moses returned to the palace that was his adopted home, Pharaoh was unable to recognize the good news, even when it was confirmed with great cost and loss of life.

Cultures often need outsiders to incarnate within them and act as a mirror to reveal their limits. Working cross-culturally, I have often found that I operate in what I can only describe as a "grace space." That is, my host cultures grant me special grace as a foreigner entering in with an open mind and heart. Cambodians, for example, did not expect me, as an "adopted son," to behave "fluently" in their culture. They held me to a different standard than they would an insider. As I moved earnestly toward the cultural space occupied by Cambodian culture, I discovered myself moving simultaneously into a space of grace between cultures. In this grace space, humor and open-mindedness prevailed, and cultural messages could be exchanged. I found, too, that in this grace space, Kingdom messages could be better received and understood. The Word of God searched both cultures, mine and my Cambodian neighbors', and gently measured them against a third culture, that of the kingdom of God.

I wonder if the more a culture sabotages itself, the more likely it is that God will want to bring in an outside change agent to liberate that culture into a fresh perspective? I wonder, for example, if American culture is so deeply ingrained with materialism that God prefers to bring outsiders into our midst to prophetically call us back to biblical values of abundance? Perhaps Bono has more leverage to call Americans to greater levels of generosity than an American celebrity would have. Can Bono see insightfully into our culture and question our lifestyles in a way that we cannot or will not see for ourselves?

Practical Considerations in the Incarnational Process

Over time, we have observed that the process of incarnating among a poor community is so nuanced to personalities, teams, contexts and objectives that there are few good rules and lots of good practice. Furthermore, many other variables weigh into the equation. How old are the missionaries? Are they married? Do they have children? There simply are too many variables to legislate lifestyle from the top. Instead, we expect the process of sub-merging to be planned by the mission team members collectively—to forge a corporate expression that factors in the four dimensions, draws upon the movement's history, follows realistic processes and is affirmed by overall community leadership.

If we lose sight of incarnational ministry as a process of careful adjustments, then we threaten our sustainability, our joy in the adventure and our relationships with our neighbors. We also risk raising the bar too high, too soon, for other team members. If we burn out, then we risk deflating the expectations of our hosts and inadvertently sending a message to would-be missionaries among the poor that it can't be done.

Leadership as Lying Down: A Reflection on John 10
Darren Prince

It is 3:30 A.M., and I'm in a rain-flooded tunnel in Golden Gate Park. I'm not sleeping, but my team is. Stretched out in green army sleeping bags, we are huddled around the glowing remains of a dying fire. We've been here for several hours already, and we have several hours left before we go. How did we get here? What are we doing? And why do I feel the need to stay awake and watch?

We are a team of six young incarnational missionaries who desire to see God's kingdom raised up among the homeless of San Francisco's Haight Ashbury youth scene. Thousands of teenagers run away every year, and thousands end up living on the streets of Hollywood, Seattle, Portland and San Francisco.

How Simple Is Simple?

Sometimes simple is anything but. Even among the Franciscans, controversy arose over what constituted the essence of simple, incarnational living.

Indeed, it is difficult to find any missionary movement among the poor in any age that did not find that a simple, incarnational lifestyle became a lightning rod for argument or controversy. These arguments can take place within missionary groups as well as outside of them.

Living simply and appropriately, while it goes to the heart of the missionary enterprise among the poor, is not a simple task. Simple living in this case does not mean easy. It can, in fact, mean

It is estimated that nearly 2,000 teenagers inhabit Golden Gate Park on any given night. Some fall asleep by getting drunk enough to pass out. Some endure the cold by warming up with a shot of heroin before bed. And some avoid sleep altogether by shooting up speed and roaming through the park all night long.

In 1999, we decided as a team that we should spend time inhabiting Golden Gate Park as well. Ministries to the homeless are plentiful, but genuine friendships with the homeless are rare. On several occasions now, we have forsaken our apartments, rolled up our sleeping bags and stayed out on the streets for as many as five days in a row. We eat at soup kitchens, we beg for spare change and we sleep wherever we can find a place that is safe and dry. We have found that when we become the invited guests of our homeless friends, our ministry becomes one of mutual hospitality and trust.

It has rained heavily all night . . . so much so that the water level on the floor of our tunnel is rising significantly.

something very difficult to do and to sustain. Therefore, it is not surprising that arguments among mission team members can arise and that, once raised, these arguments and different perspectives can take on a profoundly moral dimension. Typically, division begins when one team member criticizes another for not living "low" enough to minister authentically among the poor of their particular community. Conversely, the second team member may feel that the first is living an excessively low lifestyle purely on principle, courting unnecessary risk or inviting unnecessary fatigue, which in turn, slows down other team members.

Over time, disagreements over appropriate incarnational living can precipitate a loss of respect and confidence among

We have managed to make our camp at the tunnel's very center—the only dry area left, and the safest place to sleep for the night. From my vantage point, I can keep an eye on the rising water, watch both entrances to the tunnel and alert my teammates at the first sign of danger. I am laid out in front of my team—the first line of defense should someone enter the tunnel, and the first person to get wet when the water rises.

People have always told me that I am a leader. At times, I have mistaken that to mean that I'm the boss, or that I have control. At times, I have equated leadership with popularity and influence. But recently, I've been experiencing leadership the way Jesus demonstrated it. If you want to be great, Jesus said, learn to be the servant of all. And He said this while holding a towel in His hands just before washing the smelly feet of those who followed Him.

"I am the good shepherd," Jesus said at another time. "The good shepherd lays down his life for the sheep" (John 10:11).

teammates, can even lead to additional arguments that erupt over small issues, and can shift the group's attention from the dynamic center to the purposeless periphery. Left unchecked, without the four dimensions to provide the tools to constructively channel energies, disagreement over versions of incarnational living can raise contention to such high levels that the work suffers, missionaries leave the field in disillusionment and, ultimately, teams disintegrate.

Although this is a negative portrait, it is necessary to discuss. Incarnational living can, in its human course, go wrong. One way to keep this detour from happening is to be aware from the outset of how our human differences can complicate

He gives us a vivid picture of His style of leadership: the sheep are gathered into a cave for the night, and the shepherd literally lies down across the opening. If any harm comes to the sheep, it must pass through the shepherd first. This is truly a strange leadership posture—stretched out flat, serving as a human gate.

At nearly 4:00 A.M., the water is closer but still probably a couple of hours from reaching us. Suddenly, I hear the sound of a car and see a flash of oncoming headlights across the tunnel. Park police on routine patrol turn their car into the tunnel entrance and begin moving our way. I hurriedly wake the others, shouting, "It's time to move!" Blinded by the approaching headlights, I wave my arms frantically to ensure that the police see us. If they don't see us, they may not stop. The engine swells, then the car stops. Seconds later, it reverses out of the tunnel the way it came in. The police don't even stop to harass us or tell us to move on. We are safe. We can stay.

this process. On the other hand, the positive portrait of incarnational living is both powerful and inspirational.

A full appreciation of incarnational ministry as a model, method, message and spiritual discipline helps give practitioners a strong conceptual grip on their efforts, a durable platform from which to clarify the team's vision, and a framework to better understand the strongly held convictions that motivate each team member. The four dimensions used as a framework up front to forge a common expression of incarnational ministry help release energy to the work that otherwise might be dissipated in team conflict. Furthermore, one person believing in and living out an incarnational ministry can be dismissed by

In the panic and confusion, my wife, Pam, has accidentally rolled onto the hot coals of our dying fire. I notice the smoke coming from her sleeping bag and begin swatting at her to put it out. My team is disoriented but quickly settles back down to sleep. I'm not sure they even know what just happened. I don't even think they know that I'm staying awake to protect them. And I *know* they don't know that the foot of my sleeping bag is now at the edge of the rising water.

"I lay my life down voluntarily," Jesus said when describing His kind of leadership (v. 18). Shepherding, for Him, meant giving up His rights, privileges and well-being so that His sheep could thrive. "I have come that they may have life, and have it to the full" (v. 10). It is while lying there, in the darkness of that tunnel in Golden Gate Park, that I realize what leadership truly is. It is staying awake so that my team can sleep. It is getting wet so that they can stay dry. It is watching so that they don't have to watch. In this moment, I am painfully aware of what I

the host culture as idiosyncratic. But a missionary community living out incarnational ministry in unity cannot.

Is It Worth the Cost?

Incarnational ministry is not the only way to express good news among the poor. The rigorous adjustment process can be time-consuming and personally demanding, especially for mission workers coming from middle- or upper-middle-class backgrounds.

Aside from the problems, dangers and diseases, and the difficulties in having one's own personal and private space, perhaps the heaviest cost of incarnational ministry is choosing to identify

am giving up on their behalf—even when they don't notice it. This is the Good Shepherd's style of leadership—leadership as lying down. *

Bitter Fruit
John Hayes

In 1993, Deanna and I lived in Phnom Penh for a season. One long-time mission leader, who was a native Cambodian, told us he had never seen anyone minister alongside Cambodians the way we did, as humble learners. He shared with us the resentment he had felt growing up, relating to Western missionaries. His father had been ordained a pastor by a Western denomination but was side-lined when it came to real leadership. Although his father was counted as an important leader and positioned visibly in slide shows, he was paid much less than his Western counter-parts in Phnom Penh. He was also "expected to wash the cars and carry the luggage of the expatriate missionaries anytime they traveled." With candor and some bitterness, this leader described the villas the Western missionaries lived in and other aspects of upper-class life they enjoyed, which distanced them from common Cambodians.

Year later, I still reflect on our friend's experience. This man, his father, and doubtless many others were the fruit of godly labor several generations ago. But that fruit had come at a cost in intro-ducing a religious colonialism that lives on to this day. ✳

with only one people, one place. Choice is at the very heart of incarnation. As John Perkins used to say, nailing one's feet to the floor limits one's horizons and can feel like dedication to smallness. Acquiring authenticity and intimacy with a community takes years and precludes other options. Alhough he could have ministered incarnationally to the upper strata of Egyptian society, Moses found that he could throw in his lot credibly with only one people, his Hebrew brothers and sisters. Jesus, as multifaceted as He was, focused on the Jews, trusting that His followers would minister incarnationally to other people, other places. Incarnational ministry means giving up the heady illusion that "I can do everything" (or "anything I put my mind to.") For Western Christians especially, weaned on multiple options, the act of choosing and its consequences can be experienced as a substantial loss.

The mission field is full of examples of workers and church bodies that did not make that one choice, that are not incarnational and that stand out as foreign in host cultures. In Cambodia, many churches planted by mission agencies resemble Western churches not only in organization and style of worship, but even in their choir robes and church architecture. Often, these churches are pastored by Westerners, or nationals who have been trained in the West, who are as much a stranger to Cambodia as Cambodia is to them.

Is this bad? That depends on the perspective. At best, non-incarnational work is perceived as "different" within a culture; at worst, it appears colonial and culturally irrelevant. It is also important to note that culturally inappropriate mission models usually experience difficulty multiplying into people movements.

We have found that incarnational ministry among the poor is worth the personal cost. To be told by our neighbors, "You are one of us," is a sacred moment. However, incarnational ministry should not be entered into lightly. Understanding its four dimensions, and taking care to engage in this ministry as process, not product, goes a long way in helping mission workers stay the course and experience the fulfillment that comes with living and serving among the poor.

the other miracle

How have we lost the life in the living?

T. S. ELIOT, "THE WASTELAND"

On the last day of August 1997, in the small hours of the night, a Mercedes Benz lost control in a Paris tunnel and a woman was crushed and thrown unconscious. The world held its breath as Princess Diana lived on for a few hours, and then died. Five days later, Mother Teresa passed away peacefully in her sleep in Calcutta. Her health had been failing for years, but her indomitable spirit compelled her frail, tiny frame forward.

In the span of less than a week, the world had lost two of its most famous, beloved women. The world's expressions of grief were instantaneous and overwhelming. Both women were paid honors far beyond their stations. Diana, no longer a member of British royalty, was given the equivalent of a state funeral.

Heads of state, notables, and celebrities the world over gathered to pay tribute. In India, Mother Teresa was likewise buried with the highest official honors. She became only the third person in Indian history to be placed on the gun carriage that originally carried the body of Mahatma Gandhi—and she was not an Indian! Literally millions in that city took to the streets to try to join the funeral procession.

What were these colossal tributes about? Isaiah 58:6-8 offers an important insight.

Is not this the kind of fasting I have chosen:
to loose the chains of injustice,
and untie the cords of the yoke,
to set the oppressed free,
and break every yoke?
Is it not to share your food with the hungry
and to provide the poor wanderer with shelter—
when you see the naked, to clothe him,
 and not to turn away from your own flesh and blood?
Then your light will break forth like the dawn,
and your healing will quickly appear;
then your righteousness will go before you,
and the glory of the Lord will be your rear guard.

This passage is an anthem for those who are sub-merged in incarnational ministry because it is so generous in its promises to those who serve the poor.

"Then your light will break forth like the dawn" is one of the most awesome promises in Scripture. God speaks in simile to help us understand, but His full meaning is a mystery. Nevertheless, we believe the image describes the way in which God radiates His presence through us so that others might see something in us that makes them stop and consider. It is not the light of personal celebrity, but the light that points to its source, which is God. When we minister among the poor, those who see or learn of our work experience a resonance in the depth of their being, a calling out that this is the work of God.

History is full of examples of how God has kept His promise to shine supernatural light for those who serve the poor. One need only look at Church history to recognize that the most memorable Christians are often those who worked with, or stood for, the needy. St. Francis and St. Dominic come immediately to mind. Most school children, even, can recount something of the life of St. Francis. On the other hand, very few people, besides church scholars, can recall the name of a single pope contemporary with Francis, despite the power and influence they exercised in their day.

Mother Teresa was one of the most revered religious figures of her day. Her worldwide reputation is even more startling, considering that her work was based in a country in many ways antagonistic to the gospel and especially hostile to outside mission workers. As devout a person as Mother Teresa was, as energetic as she was in a mission most would shrink from, the volume of the applause for her life has more to do with God's promise in Isaiah 58 than it does with her unique character. When we take the homeless into our homes, clothe the naked and feed the hungry, our light breaks forth like the dawn far out of proportion to the substance or success of our work.

Many would argue that Princess Diana should not be mentioned alongside the founder of the Missionaries of Charity. But whatever might be said about Princess Diana, it can clearly be said that her light broke forth like the dawn. She was a groundbreaking humanitarian, particularly in her attention to needy children and those who suffered from AIDS. At a time when many people would not touch a person with AIDS, Diana hugged AIDS patients in public.

The Overlooked Sign

Luke's Gospel provides a New Testament perspective on the supernatural impact of working among the poor. In this passage, Jesus received a delegation from John the Baptist. Late in John's ministry, he experienced a dark moment of doubt, and he commissioned two disciples to certify that Jesus was the expected one.

> [Jesus] answered them, "Go and tell John what you have seen and heard: the blind receive their sight, the lame walk, the lepers are cleansed, the deaf hear, the dead are raised, and the poor have the gospel preached to them" (Luke 7:22, *ESV*).

At first glance, the last phrase about the poor appears to be tacked on to a catalog of miracles. Jesus seems to group apples and oranges. But Christ knew exactly what He was saying when He included proclaiming good news to the poor on

His list. As an echo of Isaiah 58, it is likely that Christ deliberately included the reference to the poor along with the obvious miracles, because working among the poor was a miracle too. Certainly it is a miracle of a different nature, but its power to confound and fascinate is similar to that of the classic miracles. Working among the poor is so upside-down, so contrary to the world's impulse of self-interest, that it has the ability to capture the imagination like light breaking forth as the dawn.

The experiences of InnerCHANGE members and other missionaries among the poor confirm this. As the years have passed and our work on the streets has gained momentum, we have found that the work has acquired acclaim out of proportion to its actual scale. We believe that ministering among the poor is "the other miracle," the overlooked sign of the Kingdom. Both Isaiah and Luke suggest that this work has the ability to impact and convict with supernatural power. Appreciating work among the poor as a miracle is a critical, sustaining motivation for mission workers among the poor. Understanding that God magnifies our light when we serve the poor allows us to persevere in ministry even though we are few in number and even though the returns on our personal investment often seem slow to come in. Moreover, the promise of Isaiah 58 allows us to go deep in a quality way in a small economy of scale, helping us pass up the urgency of the flesh to want to go big, to withstand our ego's demands for self-promotion. Finally, the power of the biblical promise in Isaiah 58 helps to offset the cost we pay to work among the poor.

Emperor Julian's Public Relations Problem

Early Church historians record that before Constantine the Great confirmed the Christian faith as the state religion in the year A.D. 313, Christianity spread rapidly through the Roman Empire, despite vicious persecution. One reason that Christianity seized upon the public imagination and many became believers was that Christians showed special concern for the needy, visited the imprisoned, established care for orphans and widows, and buried the dead. In fact, an aristocrat named Celsus ridiculed Christians for giving preference in evangelism to "contemptible people, slaves, and poor women."[33] But in these expressions of their upside-down values, the light of early Christians broke forth like the dawn. Less than a quarter-century after the Emperor Constantine allowed himself to be baptized as the last act of his life in 337, one of his successors, the Emperor Julian, tried vigorously to use all the power of his position to reinstate the old Roman imperial religion. But he found that Christianity had truly gripped the Roman people, largely because of the work Christians did among the poor. His reign lasted only two years, and he wrote bitterly of the power of the Christians' authenticity:

> Atheism [i.e., the Christian faith] has been specially advanced through the loving service rendered to strangers, and through their care for the burial of the dead. It is a scandal there is not a single Jew who is a beggar, and that the godless Galileans care not only for their own poor but for ours as well; while those who belong to us look in vain for the help that we should render.[34]

What's in It For Me?

In the 1989 movie *Field of Dreams*, Ray Kinsella (played by Kevin Costner) ploughs under much of his Iowa cornfield to build a baseball field. He does this at great personal and family sacrifice in response to a voice that tells him, "If you build it, he will come." One by one, beginning with Shoeless Joe Jackson, disgruntled baseball players come back from the dead through the cornrows beyond center field and play scratch games on Ray's field. Eventually, a reclusive writer joins Ray and his family, and Shoeless Joe invites the author to follow him and the other players into the mysteries of the cornfield. Ray is taken aback that the writer, not he, should be summoned to the cornfield after all he has done for the players. Shoeless Joe fixes Ray with a stare and asks solemnly, "What are you saying, Ray?" Ray cannot help himself and pours out, "I'm saying, What's in it for me?"

Sooner or later, on the road to Jericho, with so many needy pressing in and so few Samaritans to attend to them, it is natural, perhaps even legitimate, for the mission worker among the poor to weigh the personal sacrifices against the mission outcomes and ask God, "What's in it for me?" Some mission workers breathe the question with fear and trepidation, expecting a scolding. Others may ask God more forthrightly, with misguided and self-righteous resentment.

Either way, we believe that God does care about what's in it for us—that's part of what's in it for Him. He is a father of abundant grace who yearns to give good gifts to his children (see Matt. 7:11). He wants to usher us into the "mysteries of the cornfield," into a mature delight in His presence, first and foremost, and a fulfillment in the work itself.

Aside from promising us light like the dawn or supernatural impact in ministry, Isaiah 58:6-12 clearly describes our work among the poor as our opportunity for healthy gain, not simply our obligation. It draws together and clarifies the relationships among *four major biblical themes*, weaving them together with promises so rich that even the most cautious person asking "What's in it for me?" will go away satisfied.

Isaiah 58:

- Gives us confidence in directing us toward the kind of sacrifice God chooses

Drawing a Crowd
John Hayes

At first I thought it was about Deanna's platinum blond hair. Even as we just walked down the street, people cried out happy exclamations of wonder. Then I realized that crowds did not gather for Deanna's hair. They seemed to gather only when we stopped to do ministry, and this annoyed me. Furthermore, I was self-conscious about my language skills, and the press of the people unnerved me.

I was used to attending the poor in relative privacy, because I had become accustomed to the social norms of the U.S. But in Phnom Penh, it seemed that every time Deanna and I paused to give money to a beggar, or squat down and chat with or pray for a needy mom, traffic screeched to a halt. Crowds gathered to watch. It was almost comical. If Deanna and I were on the

- Confirms God's heart for the needy and ministry a-mong the poor as a top priority; it affirms the mission worker's yearning for significance
- Suggests that in working among the poor, we will move toward our own healing, individually and collectively
- Directs us toward that longed-for spiritual life and dynamic intimacy with the Lord

The One who confirms that it is more blessed to give than receive wants us to live full lives, not stunted lives of artificial self-sacrifice. In fact, we may be dangerous when we behave as if we can and must pour out our lives for the Lord and refuse any

busiest street and stopped for a beggar, cyclo and moto drivers would diagonally shoot across traffic to see what we were doing. Horns honked and rushing drivers shouted, but the semicircle of watchers would remain to watch these curious foreigners do the highly unusual thing of talking with the lowest in the Cambodian hierarchy.

I was a man with a mission that year in 1993. Deanna and I were acting as the advance scouts for an InnerCHANGE team we planned to deploy to Cambodia in the summer of 1994. Even in 110-degree heat, I used every minute of our two-month trip to do research, study the language, and network with Cambodian believers. Our ministry on the street was more an expression of our mercy gifting than a strategic part of our purpose.

One night in my time alone with the Lord, I carried my annoyance about the crowds to Him. I sensed that He wanted to remind me that whenever His Son acted in the Gospels, He drew a crowd. "Oh . . . that's right. Jesus rarely got privacy

personal gain. Self-denial must not be confused with self-annihilation, with pushing God and His gifts away as if living beneath our privilege were the high road. Perhaps that is why Christ reminded the Pharisees that He desires mercy, not sacrifice.

God desires to stretch before us a vision of living well—not simply living *well off*. Those of us whom God has called to work among the poor would do well to ask honestly and with a pure heart, "In ministering among the poor, what's in it for me?"

A People in Need of a Prescription

Isaiah 58:6-12 becomes more powerful in the context of verses 1 to 5. These five verses give us a portrait of the people of God

Cambodian street kid

when He ministered," I admitted. But that was not all. I felt God further remind me that crowds did not stop when Deanna and I talked with well-dressed Cambodians. They became curious only when we stopped for the poor. It hit me powerfully then, in a concrete-block room in Cambodia, that in a tiny way, God was keeping His promise to us to display supernatural light when we mingled with the poor. His light drew the crowds. ✳

as sullen and angry. They have been ritually fasting and otherwise going through the motions of religiosity, and God has shut the door of heaven on them. Verse 2 takes us to the heart of the problem from God's standpoint: "For day after day, they seek me out; they seem eager to know my ways, as if they were a nation that does what is right and has not forsaken the commands of its God"

The people complain in verse 3, "'Why have we fasted' they say, 'and you have not seen it? Why have we humbled ourselves, and you have not noticed?'"

God replies, "Yet on the day of your fasting, you do as you please and exploit all your workers. Your fasting ends in quarreling and strife, and in striking each other with wicked fists. You cannot fast as you do today and expect your voice to be heard on high. Is this the kind of fast I have chosen, only a day for a man to humble himself? Is it only for bowing one's head like a reed and for lying on sackcloth and ashes?" (Isa. 58:3-5).

This passage has a contemporary ring to it. The people's inclination is to sleepwalk their way through their devotion to the Lord. Perhaps they're doing their personal worship several times a day, saying grace at every meal, behaving with political correctness, sending their children to Christian school and buying only Christian music. They're saving the whales and supporting lobbying for Christian causes. But somehow, the blessing they are trying to arm wrestle from God keeps eluding them.

God counters through His prophet, "You drive your workers hard—I don't like your labor practices." Here and in other passages in Isaiah, we see that these same ones who are beginning to resent God for not "showing up" in their lives are oppressing the needy and unjustly amassing fortunes. Elsewhere in Isaiah, we see that they're buying second and third homes for investment purposes when some in Israel have none. Verses 3 and 4 give us a sharp glimpse of powerful business leaders squeezing the last ounce of profit from their workers. They're bowing their heads reflexively, like reeds in a cultural wind.

A Prescription for Health

Against this negative portrait, God outlines what He does want from His people in verses 6 and 7. He asks that His people work for justice, free the oppressed and feed, clothe and shelter the

Kairos
John Hayes

The veterans' hospital in Phnom Penh stands near Wat Phnom, the ancient Cambodian temple that is the historic and emotional epicenter of the city. Built in the French colonial style, the hospital looks like any number of the city's ponderous, institutional buildings from a faded era.

Deanna and I have walked by the building a number of times over the past eight or nine years; but until 1998, when Inner-CHANGE worker Dave Everitt was asked to act as chaplain there, we had no idea it was a hospital.

To step inside the Preah Kit Meleah is to step inside another world. It was built in the 1930s to offer standard, temporary care to some 700 wounded soldiers, but decades of bloodshed so uprooted families and entire communities in Cambodia that

homeless. Sounds like the profile of an activist, doesn't it?

Clearly, God confirms here that He cares about all His children, even the ones who slip through the cracks in our many human institutions and systems. He is not willing to settle for quality of life for the majority. If there is 1 desperate lamb out there, He'll leave the 99 and go in search. Looking more closely at verses 6 and 7, we find that God is not dismissing sacrifice altogether, but instead choosing a meaningful one. And incredibly, we realize that God credits ministry among the poor as a *devotional act*, not simply as a ministry activity. For those who groan at the thought of yet one more activity, the news that working among the poor doubles as a spiritual discipline, a godly fast, is great news.

in 1998, more than 1,500 veterans packed the wards as permanent residents. Many patients were single or double amputees. More than 50 percent were HIV-positive, and another 40 percent tested positive for tuberculosis. In other words, a large percentage of the men there were terminally ill.

The first time I went into Preah Kit Meleah, I expected to see the professional bustle of a vital medical center. Instead, there was a feeling of resignation and a gravity more typical of a holding facility where inmates wait to be sentenced.

Preah Kit Meleah had few staff, fewer doctors and only a handful of nurses. Because of the lack of care, about 1,400 family members crowded the halls or camped in the courtyards. They were there to cook and clean for their loved ones. Without family members to care for them, some soldiers immobilized by AIDS could lie for hours, even days, in their own contaminated bodily fluids.

Spiritual formation, including the practice of spiritual disciplines, is an important frontier for us as we seek the health of our members in groups like InnerCHANGE and UNOH (Urban Neighbors of Hope). Spiritual disciplines are also becoming a more important tool for spiritual growth in other circles as Christians seek to embrace the wisdom of the desert fathers, the Ignatian exercises, and the like. Isaiah 58:6-7 reminds us that spiritual disciplines are best done in context, one of which is among the poor.

If we examine verses 6 and 7 closely, we note that the pronouns are *"your* food, *your* clothes." Is Isaiah describing a vision for *institutional* care? No, he is speaking directly to *us,* both as indi-

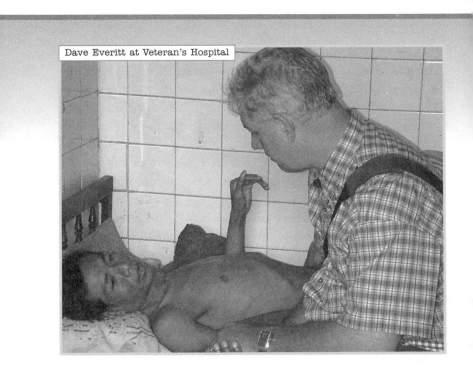

Dave Everitt at Veteran's Hospital

viduals and as communities. In our experience, we have found that the personal dimension is most often lacking in large-scale efforts to help the poor. The welfare system in the U.S., for example, is a blunt instrument that struggles to touch in a personal way. I am not suggesting that the U.S. should abandon national welfare programs for the poor. However, these programs tend to give the impression that the poor are being well cared for, which undermines incentive for substantive personal response. So the poor continue to be caught between Byzantine welfare systems and holiday food baskets.

In *A Hunger for God,* John Piper makes a great point in one of his analyses of Isaiah 58. He states that the conditionality of

In Preah Kit Meleah there is a ward for terminally ill AIDS patients called G-7. Soldiers often did not know that their skin eruptions and withering bodies were caused by AIDS until they were moved to G-7. No patient had ever walked out of G-7. The quiet terror there was punctuated by the agonies of people dying.

Dave spent most of his time on G-7. With a group of Cambodian church volunteers and a missionary from another organization, Dave patiently shared his faith and life with these men and often their wives who were also infected with AIDS.

Dave has a 250-pound, rock-climber's body, yet his gentleness and huge heart are his greatest strengths in ministry. Within the first year of ministry, more than 200 Cambodian men and women came to Christ, many of them from G-7. By 1999, more than half of these new believers had died.

A few years ago, Dave taught a Bible study with some of the new Christians in G-7 on his life verse, Romans 12:1: "Therefore

the phrasing, the "if-then," should not be read as a legalistic job description. No one can earn God's favor with right activities. Isaiah 58:6-12 should be read as a doctor's prescription for health.[35] We have seen in verses 1 through 5 that the society is sick; it has succumbed to the anesthesia of mass culture. They're into ritual, not relationship with God. And because they have fallen out of relationship with God, they have fallen into exploitative relational patterns with each other. Verses 6 through 10 are written for our well-being, not for our justification.

Isaiah 58:8 begins a remarkable series of promises that bring water to arid souls. We have talked about the promise "Then your light will break forth like the dawn" and how it

I urge you brethren, by the mercies of God, to present your bodies a living and holy sacrifice, acceptable to God, which is your spiritual service of worship" (*NASB*).

I don't know how "spiritual service of worship" translates into Cambodian, but this idea caught fire, and Dave watched in the following days as AIDS patients who were still mobile got up from their beds and began to clean and care for patients who had no one to look after them. They explained to Dave that it was their spiritual service of worship. Watching these modern-day lepers reach out to other lepers made Dave weep. In helping one another, terminally ill AIDS patients claimed back dignity from death, reminding us of the apostle Paul's cry, "O death, where is your victory?" (1 Cor. 15:55, *ESV*).

Soon afterward, Dr. Ohm Khantley, the only doctor for all of G-7, told Dave that she did not know how to fill out her monthly report to the government. Every month she implored the government to raise her budget and send her trained health-

addresses the issue of mission impact that concerns so many of us. But for those of us who struggle with dysfunction or yearn for healing, the phrase "your healing will quickly appear" comes as wonderfully refreshing news. We must not forget that this passage is written more to a people than to individuals, though we believe the power of this promise applies to both.

The next two phrases, "then your righteousness will go before you, and the glory of the Lord will be your rear guard," provide welcome news to churches that feel they are losing the integrity-image battle outside the church. When we speak to nonbelievers or those alienated by the Church, their number one criticism of the Christian community is that Christian church-

care workers. But at $20 a month no one wanted to come and perform the hazardous and grinding duty of caring for AIDS victims. She told Dave that she didn't know if she could conscionably ask the government for more help when Christians and patients themselves were providing a quality of help that money couldn't buy.

I will never forget one woman at Preah Kit Meleah, Chum Yean. As her spiritual service of worship, she offered to take care of the newborn baby of a woman who was in the last stages of AIDS and TB. Chum Yean, who had AIDS herself, promised this young mother that she would take care of the baby as long as she lived, and that when she died, her mother would care for the child. The baby was undersized and had those big eyes that AIDS children often have. I never saw Chum Yean put the baby down, and Dave told me that she lavished her with the care of two mothers.

By the end of 2001, hundreds of Christians emerged from Preah Kit Meleah. Those who survived returned to their villages.

goers are hypocrites. Whether or not this is a fair estimation of Christian attitudes is not the issue. What is important is that a reputation for hypocrisy among Christians is purportedly keeping a substantial number of people out of churches.

Isaiah 58:8 addresses this loss of reputation by saying that God credits His people with visible integrity and gifts them with His personal glory when they simply work among the poor. He watches our backs—our most vulnerable side. Few of us have heard this kind of prescription preached for the dynamic health and restoration of reputation. Sadly, instead of addressing the needs of the poor and allowing God to guard our image and reputation, we strive after it in our own strength, alternately binge-

Dave has stayed in touch with as many as he could to see that they had support to be change agents in their communities. Dave also has been instrumental in recruiting a medical doctor to work at the hospital full-time. He is an American military doctor who was paralyzed in the Gulf War. Together Dave and the doctor have recruited work teams to rehabilitate and rebuild an entire wing of the hospital and bring some of the most advanced medical care to Cambodia.

A lot has happened to advance the Kingdom at Preah Kit Meleah. But ministry among the poor always operates on borrowed time. Economic pressures, legislation or simple necessity constantly force the poor to relocate. Beginning in the autumn of 2001, while the world focused on the terrible tragedy of New York's twin towers collapsing, another smaller tearing down was taking place in Phnom Penh. The Cambodian government issued orders to demobilize Preah Kit Meleah Hospital. In March 2002, the last of the surviving soldiers and their families were

ing on performance and purging on piety.

One way to measure the truth of the promises in Isaiah 58 in contemporary experience is to track how people give their money. When we "vote" with our income, we validate that the organization we are giving to is a worthy cause. Few outside the faith will give to religious works such as church planting, but many will give to religious work among the poor. In fact, non-profits that work among the poor, both Christian and secular, consistently top the list of agencies receiving funds. For example, in both Australia and the U.S., the Salvation Army receives more donations than any other organization. The Salvation Army's righteousness goes before them.

sent back to their villages with no money to help ease the transition.

We had the privilege of being able to make the most of a unique opportunity in Cambodia. A lot happened, but a lot didn't happen, too. Of the 1,400 family members present in the late 1990s, about 400 to 500 children under age 12 lived at Preah Kit Meleah. Nearly all had never been to school and spent their days roaming the corridors and courtyards in packs, foraging for food and toys among the discarded surgical supplies. We dreamed of using the upper floor of the new wing to provide schooling and activities for these children. I shared this hope both in the U.S. and in Australia, and while people were always moved, no one was able to step forward and seize the opportunity.

Kairos is the New Testament Greek word for "divine opportunity." These are the unplanned-for and unexpected moments that call for decision and immediate action. Preah Kit Meleah

Verse 9 begins, "Then you will call, and the Lord will answer; you will cry for help, and he will say: Here am I." For many Christians, this promise is the climax of Isaiah 58. Most of us long for the dynamic spiritual life that intimacy with God brings, yet few of us go to the poor to find that company. Instead, we try to "Bible study" or "small group" our way to closeness with God. As members of incarnational ministry, we are not discounting small groups. Rather, we are trying to bring these essential elements into perspective with the prescription in Isaiah 58. The theme that we get close to God through nearness to the poor is echoed often in Scripture, most notably in Matthew 25. Jeremiah 22:16 gives us another example: "He

was a divine moment for us. We knew from the beginning that it would be hard work that would tear up our emotions. In committing Dave to this task, we committed our best evangelist and one of our most seasoned members in Cambodia. God met us there and allowed us to see great impact. But we were never able to mobilize to meet all the opportunities, and eventually the window closed. Paul, in his letter to the Galatians, wrote, "And let us not grow weary of doing good, for in due season we will reap, if we do not give up. So then, as we have opportunity [kairos], let us do good to everyone, and especially to those who are of the household of faith (Gal. 6:9-10, ESV).

Preah Kit Meleah leaves me with mixed emotions. It serves to remind me that we must seize some opportunities even if we are not fully prepared for them. On the other hand, I know that if I go back into Preah Kit Meleah and see the upper floor we were setting aside for the children, I will see opportunity lost. ✳

defended the cause of the poor and needy and so all went well. 'Is that not what it means to *know me?*' declares the Lord" (emphasis added).

As we work among the poor, we must be careful with our own expectations and balance all these promises against a full biblical backdrop of health. We do not believe that serving the poor is the silver bullet that magically resolves all our problems. Nor do we recommend engaging the needy simply to wrest blessing from God. But there is something about the reality of ministering among the poor that both reveals our real issues and helps direct us toward the kind of grace we need to grow. The point is that few of us have been taught that serving the poor is a divine means for our own health, individually and corporately. Also, we do not have many role models who can mentor us in this regard, and the ones we do have we tend to put out of reach as saints whose spirituality is loftily beyond us.

If working among the poor is so supernatural an expression of light and so powerful a prescription for health, and steers us closer to God, why do so few of us engage the poor? When congregations find themselves sagging in authenticity and their reputations suffer, why do they not turn to Isaiah 58 for direction? We pay a heavy price as God's people for our neglect of the poor—a price that goes beyond the tragic social and political costs of poverty. We pay a spiritual price. Across our lands, around the world, as we neglect the poor, we may find ourselves sighing deeply and asking God, "Why have we fasted and You have not seen? Why have we humbled ourselves and You have not noticed?"

submitting

"Why do my eyes hurt?"
"You've never used them before."

NEO QUESTIONING MORPHEUS, *THE MATRIX*

I shrug off the first sound, eager to remain asleep. The second sound is sharp and sinister. I yank my body upright, staring into blackness with the listening eyes of the blind. There is nothing but an echo's remains and the torn wing of an interrupted dream.

My mind sifts rapidly through frame after frame of images in which I confront drug dealers breaking into my apartment on Minnie Street. Finally, like a TV cop, I get up and fling open the bedroom door in order to catch any intruders off guard. But there is no one. I am grateful, and feel embarrassed, as if I'd been seen overreacting.

Missteps and Misunderstandings

On December 2, 1986, miscommunications on my part and that of the Santa Ana police led tar heroin dealers living across the street to conclude that I was a police informer. That Saturday, I awoke in a fog. We had had a late night with Cambodian youth the night before. So it wasn't until 10:30 that morning that I wandered out to our balcony.

Crowds of neighbors lined the street. Several plainclothes policemen and an officer or two in uniform had blocked off the street and were talking earnestly with one another, arms folded. Three young Latino males, bandanas wound around their heads, were handcuffed on the curb, under guard. Two more officers wearing sunglasses chatted in the middle of the street. One had his foot on the head of a young man sprawled awkwardly on the ground, as if resting it casually on a stone.

I was incensed that the police would make so deliberate a show of callous authority on our street. I recognized a few of the young men in cuffs as fairly new arrivals to Minnie Street, men who spoke little English and got caught up quickly in the drug trade. They drove a souped-up powder-blue VW. A few nights before, rival dealers had shattered their windshield. Crack had just begun to ramp up on our street, so with new money to be made on new product, Minnie Street was experiencing an increase in traffickers.

Without thinking clearly, I approached the officers at the curb and asked them if the two officers in the middle of the street needed to be so brutal in their arrest. Immediately the two officers whirled on me. One pulled a small spiral notebook and pen out of his pocket, took the cap off with his mouth and through clenched teeth asked me who I was, where I lived and what my connection with the young men was. I quickly cleared up the confusion, and the officers in the street relaxed and then shoved the young men into the parked squad cars. I got into my car a bit shaken and began rethinking what I had done. I remember looking up at my neighbor's apartment and glimpsing Suth Chai and his family squeezed into the window, with expressions of real concern on their watchful faces.

It was the first of several less-than-circumspect encounters with the police. In my early years on Minnie Street as a single man, I took, perhaps, a more proprietary stance on my neighborhood than God was asking me to. But this particular incident was regrettable for the message it sent to the friends and family of the young Latino men, who suspected I was informing on them rather than asking the police for better treatment.

Being labeled a "rat" on Minnie Street carried potentially grave consequences. In November, a Cambodian man who had agreed to be a block captain in a novel police initiative was reportedly shot to death at night in his bed. On a racially divided street, I had been perceived not only as having sided with Cambodians, but also now to work with the police. Suddenly, it seemed to me that Latino men all over the street were monitoring my movements and attempting to stare me down. My instincts told me to stay outside and move freely. If I were skidding toward confrontation, it would be easier to deal with out on the street in broad daylight. The word "rat" was traced in the dust on my windshield, and late at night there was strange activity at my door designed to unnerve me.

My instincts told me that if I left, I'd have to leave for good. On the other hand, the first couple of days after this incident, it was impossible not to second-guess my resolve to stay. From 1985 until 1988, and again in 1992, killings occurred fairly regularly on Minnie Street. Was I stubbornly insisting on a battle that the enemy had staged? Was I not responsible for my carelessness with police officers for jeopardizing the work God entrusted to us? Could I not, in fact, move to another poor neighborhood, start over and proceed more wisely?

I prayed more than ever before. This urgent turn of events had broken any last vestiges of formality between God and me. There are times when our dependence on God becomes so palpably transparent that we can only lean into Him. In a free-fall moment of grace, God kicked out any false floors built on cherished notions of who I thought I was, wished to be or should be. This was about His will, not my skill. I realized that incarnating on Minnie Street had been a God-designed process that intimately wove me into the living tissue of a community dear to Him. I sensed that He was quietly offering me the privilege of re-choosing Minnie Street, not simply as ministry target, but as home. I chose to stay.

After four days of playing psychological chess with dealers and their sympathizers, I found myself walking home alone at dusk after playing pick-up ball with neighborhood youth at the elementary school. Basketball in hand, I came to the north opening of Minnie Street, off Wakeham, and started bouncing the ball furiously down the middle of the street. If anyone were to come at me from under cover of parked cars, I'd detect this better from the middle of the street. Near my apartment, I found four dealers leaning back on the blue VW, arms folded, smiling and waiting for me.

"Hey, rat!" one of them sneered, with a classic street head nod. Praying, I walked over to the group. I zeroed in on the leader and disciplined myself not to look right or left. To do so confirms for a gang its strength in number. Amazingly, all four began to back up. The leader knew he was on the spot, and he knew there was no script for what was to come.

In a torrent of English and Spanish, I gushed out my intention to stay on the street. I didn't even attempt to deny that I had been an informer for the police. That seemed irrelevant.

I blurted out, "This street isn't yours or mine. It belongs to Jesus." I remember closing with, "I am with the church. I came here to love this street, not to fight on it." Three of the dealers

Whose Cup?
John Hayes, April 1986, Minnie Street

A fine mist falls, enough to bleed the dust on my windshield. It is nearly midnight on a Friday. The light from my headlights picks out a form here and there as I cruise the corridor of parked and abandoned cars. A prostitute poses provocatively. Huddles of heroin and crack dealers break instantly and position themselves, peering intently into my car. Some recognize me. Some don't and try to flag me down for a transaction.

In my rearview mirror a figure races after me. I ease into a space close to my complex and roll down the window as the young Latino man catches up to me.

"You looking for something?" he asks suggestively.

"No." Our eyes lock. "I live here."

started to melt into the shadows between apartment complexes, tossing out parting words in Spanish that I had not seen in my Spanish Bible. The leader blinked convulsively and finally walked with firm dignity between the buildings toward the parking lot. He never said a word. And I never saw those four again on Minnie Street. I had gotten the impression they lived there, but I never saw them or their distinctive car again.

As I walked up the steps of my building, I was breathing as if I were climbing down from a high altitude. It was now dark. Inside, I leaned against my front door and slid to the floor laughing. "I came here to love this street . . ." Somehow, that was not the kind of phrasing I'd expected God to pour through me to

"Oh. I thought . . . yeah, you live here." He looks both disappointed and doubtful.

"I drive through here everyday. You've never seen me?" I toss out impatiently.

"Hey, I never seen you man." He backs away, palms thrust outward, pushing air. "I never seen you, okay?"

I stay in the car a moment with the window down. The pavement is damp, not wet enough to cleanse, but moist enough to raise the smell of stale beer, urine and chewing gum baked black. It is not an entirely unwelcome smell to me, as it kindles the fresh scent of calling.

I step out, crunching fragments of shattered windshield. Trash spills from an overflowing dumpster, and fast-food wrapping gusts at my feet. The laundry room door of my apartment complex is ajar. I step past the door to grab the railing of our steps, glance back into the washroom and glimpse a hypodermic needle plunging into a tied-off, tautened forearm.

tough dealers. When He promised in His Word to prepare us with the right words at the right times in crises, I expected something a little more sophisticated. But who was I to quibble? I had the sense that God enjoyed my reaction. All the same, I deeply appreciated how He had orchestrated that interaction out on the street.

Minnie Street, 1985-1992

My experience in December 1986, wrestling with dealers for permanent footing on Minnie Street, allowed me to re-choose Minnie Street. It also compelled me to revisit and reevaluate the journey. I felt rescued for purpose, and this helped to renew our

Minnie Street

small team with a sense of purpose as well. Instead of restlessly moving ahead to get the job done, as if time existed only ahead of me, I began to more prayerfully journal the experience behind me. When we worked reflectively, we realized that we were gaining insights that could be valuable handholds and footholds for future teams among the poor in other places.

Finding My Incarnational Place

Minnie Street was several blocks long with no intersecting side streets. It wasn't part of Orange County's grid pattern, wasn't on the way to anything. The street was lined with two-story, horseshoe-shaped apartment complexes. Most of the courtyards

Next morning, I awake and hardly know myself; I am so stirred with clashing emotions. April marks my first anniversary of moving to the street, and though I am grateful for the transformation I have seen in relationships on the Cambodian side of Minnie Street, I am keenly aware of my incapacity to impact the Latino side. I am especially cognizant of the untouched drug subculture. Though the dealers on Minnie Street are Latino, almost to a man, combined with the users, the drug culture actually represents a third "equal-opportunity" group. The image from inside the washroom of the night before lingers like the chalk outline of a body.

In choosing to incarnate into the Cambodian life in my neighborhood, to immerse in its language and culture, I have unintentionally confirmed a non-choice on the Latino side. Is my experience half-full or half-empty? I sit on my mattress on the floor and pray. I start with fierce prayer warfare against the *personal* evil of substance abuse, and imagine a crashing sound

were concrete; a few were dirt and grass. Two-thirds of the residents were Latino immigrants, largely undocumented, who had lived on Minnie Street an average of two to three years. One-third were Cambodian refugees, most from rural farming backgrounds. Some had arrived as early as 1981. Most had been there a year or more. Cambodians were still coming, and there was a sense among the Latino population that Cambodians were going to tip the balance and take control of the street.

I first found Minnie Street on foot, partly by the smell of sewage and rotting jacaranda blossoms. I quickly discovered that there were no churches nearby. (Only one church, Trinity Presbyterian, had Minnie Street on its radar.)

in the heavenlies. Eventually, I segue into a stream-of-consciousness venting of frustration. I realize I had expected to see more ministry results by this time.

I cannot get Psalm 23 out of my mind. "My cup runneth over," I repeat to myself again and again, quoting the *King James Version* as a way of crawling back into the lap of childhood. Gradually, I sense that I am being invited to lift my eyes above the cup of ministry outcomes, half-full or half-empty. Instead I am drawn to focus on the One who fills the cup. ✳

I felt that this street was small enough to get my arms around. It felt to me like a place I could "nail my feet to the floor," as John Perkins had suggested I look for, back in December 1984.

After working in South Central Los Angeles, John was the person and mentor who gently pushed me to consider starting again in a new neighborhood where I could begin as a learner and put down "incarnational DNA." The day John shared this insight with me is a day I now consider a divine appointment. Over the years, intersecting with him personally, and drawing insight from the CCDA movement (Christian Community Development Association), he has become one of the most significant mentors of my life.

Courting the Street

I relocated to Minnie Street only after a lengthy courtship, partly by design, partly by necessity (it took months to find an apartment in this overcrowded block). I began to weave relationally into networks of Cambodian families and study their language. I purposely studied language in homes and on front lawns so that I could be seen as a learner and a son. Like Jesus in His incarnational trajectory, I needed to grow up in the culture. I also wanted to communicate that I was not looking to come in primarily as an outside service provider. I test-drove a few Bible clubs with the children, most of whom could be reached in English, but always with the permission of families, and usually inside homes.

I moved to 1014 South Minnie Street one Friday night. My apartment had no power or running water. My landlord, a management firm that rented most of the apartments on the street, had asked me to wait until the following week to relocate. But I was so eager to be on site that I moved in the first day I could. Rotting carpet had been pulled up in most of the front room, leaving behind an evil smelling glue and thorny carpet tacks. Besides a bedside lamp and mattress, and two armfuls of clothes, I had next to nothing, so I was able to move in a single trip in a friend's van. What I *did* have were boxes of books. I picked out college texts I'd loathed in my student days and used them as stepping stones to cross the front room.

Holy Ground

A cloud of neighbors hovered at my front door. Suth Chai, who lived in apartment 6, came into my apartment with a proprietary air, signaling to the others that I was his responsibility. He was hauling an extension cord he used to hook up my lamp in the bedroom. His wife, Thong Dam, came carrying gallon jugs of water. It was late Friday night by the time I had my mattress down and clothes hung. I stowed the rest of my book boxes in a smelly dark closet. My neighbors went back to their apartments, but all around me I could hear the murmur of teeming life. The fat black extension cord that ran like an umbilical cord from Suth Chai's apartment into mine meant that we could not fully close our front doors, and I was indebted to my neighbor for his willingness to risk safety for new friendship.

I was so electric with anticipation for the next day of "ministry" that I was still wide awake at 3:00 A.M., and I took out my journal and Bible and sifted through the book of Joshua to refresh myself with insights about scouting out new land. I sensed God nudging me out the door, reminding me that I couldn't explore or prayer-walk from inside, so I rushed out into the night. Minnie Street was still, so I headed for the back parking lot. In its abandoned cars and shadows, dealers and prostitutes were still carrying on business. Crunching broken glass underfoot, reading graffiti and tags on walls, I began to pray. A prostitute who was slithering out of her work clothes between parked cars nodded to me, and some young men drinking beer glanced twice at me, as if making sure I was real.

I prayed as I walked. I engage in some of my deepest prayer in motion. The night was less fearful than sacred. I remember an impulse to take off my shoes because the ground felt so holy.

I learned that night and in similar nights since that praying as one walks through a neighborhood is a powerful experience, and combined with a "courtship," helps bring fullness to one's entry into a neighborhood so that one feels less like a stranger moving in. Prayer-walking Minnie Street helped confirm for me that in approaching every new poor community, we step onto holy ground. In the 1980s, I was schooled to think of poor neighborhoods as war zones that needed to be fixed, and quickly. In my first few months living on and courting Minnie Street, I realized that this impression was not only superficial, but it was also disempowering.

Complexities, Insights and Urgent Prayers

I quickly learned that Minnie Street had as much in common with two-thirds-world communities as it did with American inner-city "hoods." During the day, Minnie Street was flush with Cambodian and Latino families, and its active networks functioned as a village. By night, Minnie Street gave way to inner-city individualism, with dealers and users coming in from other parts of Santa Ana to stake out the back parking lot. In the liminal space between day and night, one gang or another would often stalk the street.

One of the strategic decisions I had to make in the early days was to focus. This was hard to do. I was drawn to and fascinated by everyone on the street. Focusing was only preliminarily about choosing between Latinos and Cambodians. It was also about deciding whether to minister within the two-thirds-world village by day and penetrate the gang culture in the evenings or relate to the "hood" by night.

I chose to work among the networks of Cambodian families. I then had to confront the reality that the Cambodians were not one group, but three. There were Cambodian elders, parents and grandparents whose heart and only language were Cambodian. Then there were their older sons and daughters, ranging in age from late teens to early twenties. I called this group Cambodian Americans, because their heart language was Cambodian, but the world they were breaking into was transacted in English. They were often out of the house, as they were the primary bread-winners, typically working at fast-food restaurants. Finally, there were the American Cambodians, elementary-age children whose best and preferred language was English. Often, children were their parents' translators; but just as often, the children could not fully understand the language of their parents. After several months of living on Minnie Street, celebrating weddings, attending funerals and eating in homes, I sensed friction developing between the generations in Cambodian households, and it grieved and challenged me.

It quickly became apparent to me that children and youth were already at risk. Cambodian youth were gravitating to gangs, alcohol and, to a degree, drugs. Both children and youth were feeling pressures that their parents could not relate to and didn't always have the language to address.

Confronting the complexity in the Cambodian village, and sensing that time was an accelerating factor in dividing families, I believed that Minnie Street would be best served missionally if others came in to help. I began by looking for people in the Latino and Cambodian churches I attended across town. I also looked to members of Trinity Presbyterian. Slowly, God began to bring volunteers, but it was clear that the dangers and intricacies of Minnie Street were a tall order for them. Crack made its debut on the street, and our back lot became more dangerous than ever.

I am not sure when I first began to pray earnestly for God to bring the street better people than me. I am not sure how many days, weeks or months I prayed this before I felt God enter my room. I sensed Him asking me if I really meant what I was praying, and that if He answered my prayer, it might be rough on my ego. That made sense. It might be hard for me to give way to better people, especially as the pioneer. Images of the street began to flash through my mind: neighbors struggling with terrible diseases, missing limbs, suffering from post-traumatic stress disorder as a result of decades of war in Cambodia—and that was just the Cambodian side. Clearly, the street needed deeply spiritual and deeply skilled missionaries. So I told the Lord, "Yes, I am serious." I trembled when I said, "Bring this street better people than me, holy people." I also remember Him suggesting that perhaps what the Cambodians needed more than holy people was a holy God.

Stuart Murray, in *Church after Christendom,* writes, "Mission originates in the character and creation-wide purposes of God, not in the church. . . . 'Missional church' does not mean churches embracing mission more enthusiastically but encountering afresh the missionary God."[36] Some volunteers were coming in several times a week and were more passionate about the street than they were about their jobs and even their local churches. Most came looking for mission to add to and enrich their lives. Instead, they encountered the missionary God, and their work on Minnie Street ceased to be extracurricular. They found themselves constantly thinking and praying about families on the street, regardless of the number of hours they could commit. Some transitioned to full-time staff. Others remained regular volunteers for years. It was humbling and inspiring to watch God evoke this level of faithfulness in people.

Chosen by the Children

My first strategic instinct was to begin relationships and ministry with the adults on Minnie Street, but to be as available to the at-risk children and youth as I could be. However, the children on the street decided to begin with me. Children of all ages came to my apartment. I invested in art supplies and that brought more children in. Over time, they leaned on my sliding glass windows so hard and so often that the fixtures came loose and the glass could be carefully lifted out and placed to the side. Often I'd wake to the sound of the smallest children in my front room. Occasionally, I'd hear them singing songs from our Bible clubs.

As God brought more volunteers and eventually full-time staff, I was able to focus more and more on the children. This informal decision got an unexpected boost from the Cambodian families themselves. I discovered from my Cambodian friend Sari Keo, that as a single man ministering full-time, I was considered the monk in the neighborhood. Many families encouraged their children to come to my house for Bible clubs in the same way they would have encouraged their children to go to the Wat (temple) in their homeland. Within the first six months, numbers of children became Christians.

Finally, we had to be very flexible, exploring and adjusting strategies that fit. We were on our knees a lot as we so often wondered how to proceed. Strategically, the most important source for our direction was unquestionably the four Gospels. In fact, it felt like Jesus drew us into the Gospels and shut the door behind us. We hungered for Jesus not only as Savior but also as mission leader, and carefully weighed Scripture passages for practical insights.

What Is Your Model?

"What is your model?" I am occasionally asked.

In the early years I used to struggle somewhat in responding to this question, because each city in which we had teams followed a unique blueprint. And even within cities, team members were often using more than one model of empowerment to realize the potential of a neighborhood. Eventually, I realized this was as it should be. We *should* expect each city, each work, to look different as it reflects the unique genetic code of hopes and aptitudes present among the poor and among our team members. If every city followed the same model and scheduled the same steps toward an outcome of church planting or jobs creation or community development, how flexible could we be in satisfying the agenda of the poor themselves?

We use multiple models, depending on the type of ministry we engage in, drawing on wisdom from a variety of sources. We have found, however, that the genre of biblical story is universally effective. As much as possible, we weave curriculum and story together in a dynamic we call "story-basing." Certainly Church history has shown the Bible to be an exceptionally accessible book culturally, and the fact that it is 80 percent story con-tributes to that accessibility.

For our models to be both culturally appropriate and powerful, they have to be memorable. Nearly all cultures find story accessible, attractive and eminently memorable. People who struggle to recall the 5 Ss of leadership, the 10 values of church planting, and whose eyes glaze over at flowcharts can easily retell the Good Samaritan parable.

Because we spent so much time in the Gospels as a community, not surprisingly we began to use Gospel stories as scaffolding for curriculum that could be used by emerging local leaders.

Our formation materials are largely oral, dialogue-driven and low-tech—yet profound. The story of four friends taking a paralyzed man to Christ in Mark 2 became one of our foundational training vehicles. Like most good stories, Mark 2 can be distilled to just a few memorable images in a single sitting. Or it can be stretched as a conceptual framework in an overarching way for several training sessions. I will stretch the story here to indicate how expansive it can be in absorbing curricular insights.

A few days later, when Jesus again entered Capernaum, the people heard that he had come home. So many gathered that there was no longer room, not even outside the door, and he preached the word to them. Some men came, bringing to him a paralytic, carried by four of them. Since they could not get him to Jesus because of the crowd, they made an opening in the roof above Jesus and, after digging through it, lowered the mat the paralyzed man was lying on. When Jesus saw their faith, he said to the paralytic, "Son, your sins are forgiven."

Now some teachers of the law were sitting there, thinking to themselves, "Why does this fellow talk like that? He's blaspheming! Who can forgive sins but God alone?"

Immediately Jesus knew in his spirit that this was what they were thinking in their hearts, and he said to them, "Why are you thinking these things? Which is easier: to say to the paralytic, 'Your sins are forgiven,' or to say, 'Get up, take your mat and walk'? But that you may know that the Son of Man has authority on earth to forgive sins . . ." He said to the paralytic, "I tell you, get up, take your mat and go home." He got up, took his mat and walked out in full view of them all (Mark 2:1-11).

Understand the Nature of the Work / Mission

Perhaps the first thing to note is the condition of the man the four friends carry to Jesus. Mark calls him a paralytic. Left to himself, he is not likely to find his way to Christ.

There are streets, neighborhoods and, indeed, whole communities that, like this man, are paralyzed in some way. Poverty deriving from political oppression, unemployment, substance abuse, crime, gangs and/or inadequate Christian witness—all these separately or together can so immobilize a community that left to itself it is not likely to see Kingdom transformation. A paralyzed community needs tangible help, as this man in Mark 2 needed help. There is more here than a story of four men carrying a paralytic to Christ. This story can also reveal to us our attitudes about the poor and about ourselves as mission agents. I find aspects of Luke's account more comfortable to my culturally sensitive ears. In the *New American Standard Version* of the Bible, a version noted for its accurate word choice, Luke describes the man afflicted as a "man who was paralyzed" (Luke 5:18). To twenty-first-century ears, Mark's use of the word "paralytic" appears dangerously close to seeing the man as a stereotype—a paralytic, not a human being who is paralyzed. Stereotypes limit the imagination, and thus limit potential. Is Mark wrong to use this word "paralytic"? Not necessarily. As Jews of their time, Matthew, Mark and John all use this kind of categorical language, and the paralyzed man probably saw himself as a paralytic. I wonder, though, if it is possible that in Luke's choice of words, he demonstrates that we should strive to discern the person apart from a condition.

We Assume Attitude

This biblical story can be used to bring to the surface our essential attitudes toward those in need. Is there a man apart from the disease, or is the disease the overriding characteristic—the bottom line? Do we refer to poor communities simply in their aggregate needs: substandard housing, AIDS in epidemic proportion, inadequate water and hygiene, unemployment? Or do we describe them as communities of families: men, women and children, all with hopes and dreams, hemmed in by physical and economic limits? The archetypal faces of poverty can obscure the personal faces of the poor.

Missionaries can spring into action in response to a need, *assuming* they have an empowering attitude; but in their haste to meet needs, they communicate that getting to the problems is more critical than getting to know the poor themselves and working together toward solving the problems. When missionaries start with the need, hoping they will one day get to know poor people personally, they are likely to be found 10 years later, still addressing the need. They are welcome, even necessary, outsiders, but outsiders nonetheless. On the other hand, when mission workers start with poor people in empowering relationships, they are likely to get to the problems, together with the poor. The "work" typically starts slower and looks less impressive when relationship is prioritized before attention to the need, but it is more likely to be owned and reproduced by the poor themselves and, as a result, have a much longer lifespan.

Just because the paralyzed man is not likely to get to Christ alone does not mean he is less valuable, less human, than others in the story walking on their own. All desperately need Christ.

Organize for Action

A second useful concept in Mark's story is that the four friends are organized for action. They possess a Jesus-style faith, integrating words and deeds. They are willing both to carry the man to Jesus (as opposed to simply preaching to him) and to tear up the roof. Obvious as this point is, imagine for a moment that one of these four men has prioritized word over work, fearing that holism might diminish evangelistic fervor. As the team considers opening up the roof, he balks, saying, "I don't do projects; I just preach the word." Mark's story might have ended differently.

We are committed to expressing the kingdom of God in needy neighborhoods in both word and work, in holistic union.

Attend to Preparation

The third component we find in Mark's Gospel account is attentiveness to preparation. Four men gather to carry the man, exact-

Giving Back
Tammy Fong Heilemann, Kampong Cham, Cambodia

June 1 was International Children's Day, a day to pause and celebrate the gift that children are to the world. For our 17 young women at the House of Hope, all former prostitutes, their childhood was compromised. Many of our girls were sold or manipulated by their families into the commercial sex trade. A few were kidnapped into it. Still others were lured into prostitution for the money. Many of the girls arrive at House of Hope with TB, AIDS or both; all come with deep emotional scarring.

On November 16, 1998, we officially opened the House of Hope in Kampong Cham City with two girls who had escaped the trade by jumping out of their hotel window. Our facility is full at 20 girls; but with the pressing need, we occasionally take in a few more. House of Hope is designed to be a two-year residential

ly the number to manage every corner of a stretcher. They had to make plans and communicate in order to decide who would lead and who would carry in back. All of this is mundane but should not be taken for granted. The opening act of living and ministering in a neighborhood includes much that feels mundane, such as countless hours practicing the language, observing cultural patterns, praying, listening and more listening. All of this is vitally necessary.

If we miss the preparation that leads to healing in Mark's story, we are likely to miss this in our own stories as we set about to move into a poor community missionally.

When Christians mobilize in American inner cities without considering the many ordinary aspects of sub-merging—without

program in which we give the girls the opportunity to reclaim their lives by teaching them a trade and exposing them to the love of Christ. A value we try to instill in the girls is giving. Despite the horror and abuse they have experienced, we show the girls that they can be more than victims, and that giving back in some way can help them regain their dignity.

International Children's Day offered our girls a chance to give back to children who are even needier than they are. We suggested that they go with us to visit Kampong Cham's orphanage. When our social workers sketched the vision of expressing love to the orphans, many of whom had been abandoned, some of the girls cried. But they drew a blank when we asked them what they had to give to the orphans. Did they really have nothing to give? Finally, one of the girls suggested they could give the orphans some of the money they earned cutting hair and sewing. Other girls joined in enthusiastically, and soon it was decided to buy school supplies for the children and make 400 cakes. The girls

courting the neighborhoods—the work suffers.

Four men carried the pallet—enough but not too many. Mark suggests that there were more men accompanying the four, but only four actually served as bearers. Often poor communities are fragile ecosystems. Too many mission leaders living too close together can inadvertently blunt the emergence of leaders from the neighborhood itself.

Build Community

The fourth lesson we draw from this story is that it takes a community to reach a community. It would have been impossible to take the paralyzed man to Christ if the four men were not in

Tammy (right) at House of Hope

sync or if they wanted to pursue the task in individualistic fashion. What if they let a squabble as they were carrying the man disrupt them? What if one dropped out and there were too few to carry the stretcher? The probability would be that the paralyzed man would never get to Christ, and the stretcher-bearers would go home in anger and confusion.

In my experience, mission works best as an ensemble rather than a solo affair. It is strategic for the host community, for the man on the stretcher, and for the support and ongoing formation of the team members. I find that the most effective teams in mission among the poor understand that community is not simply a touch-base event once a week in which to gather for

worked as a group to bake the little cakes, singing worship songs as they wrapped them in banana leaves.

On June 1, all of our young women and most of our Cambodian staff headed to the orphanage to share the goodness and blessings they had received from the House of Hope. They dressed up, many proudly wearing the new purple skirts and white blouses they had sewn themselves. They were so excited! We toured the government facility, and some of our girls cried when they saw how young some of the children were.

After a ceremony in which one of our more mature girls poignantly shared about our intent in coming to visit the orphanage, the girls handed out the small gifts and led the children in a fun game outside. It was a lovely day. Our young women, who have known terrible suffering but are now rebuilding their lives, were able to see that they could encourage others by giving from their hearts. That day, they discovered that it is indeed more fulfilling to give than to receive. ✳

support so that they can go back out and do "their" ministry individually. Community involves the deep exploration of the gifts, natural abilities and acquired skills of individual team members who are working to combine them in synergy.

Commit to the Process

Despite the resolve of the four friends and the paralyzed man to get to Christ, they arrive after the place in which Jesus is ministering is already crowded—so crowded that they cannot enter through the door. It's as if they had traveled in the breakdown lane. Able-bodied citizens who could make it to Christ on their own, or perhaps simply those who lived closer, had already filled the space to overflowing. I imagine that after the planning and execution of getting to Jesus, the five confronted the crowded doorway stunned and heartbroken.

Nowadays, most churches that run out of seating space go to multiple services or embark on building projects. It is a hard fact for the poor and for those called to serve among them that few churches prioritize funds for the poor before internal concerns. In the same way, it must have been hard for the five men to get to the blocked door and find no one willing to budge. Were the people crowding the door "bad" people? I think, in Mark's story at least, the crowd is behaving with the singular mind-set of individuals all clamoring to be with Jesus. A church could have worse problems.

As mission teams among the poor, we have two options, and we must be prepared to exercise both. The first option is to stand at the door of the church and cry out for justice on behalf of the poor—to ask the mainstream to open the floor to critical resources that allow disabled communities to gain access to Jesus. The second is to go to the roof and take the lid off the system. The first option can be difficult, demoralizing work, because as many workers among the poor have discovered, we are admired when we work with the poor in mercy; however, we are often avoided when we work as prophets on their behalf. Yet we have to be prepared to answer the calling of Jesus in this regard, because prophetic ministry is as much about seeking justice for the unjust and the unaware as it is about seeking justice for the denied. I find it curious that in this story, Jesus does not condemn the crowd for not moving aside to let the five men enter. Neither can we slip from prophetic expression into condemnation. On the other hand, notice that Jesus also does not condemn the four friends for tearing up the roof. Kingdom justice and mercy are both perfectly served in this account as only Jesus can accomplish. The paralyzed man was mercifully healed. In addition, Jesus quietly served notice to the mainstream crowd that the last are first and the needy are blessed as He attended immediately to the paralyzed man, despite the fact that he was the last to arrive.

Create Innovative Strategies

If ever there was an upside-down way to get to Jesus, those men found it. They circumvented the crowd, got to the roof, created an opening, and lowered the man to the floor.

In a right-side-up world, mission communities working among the poor, despite their most eloquent prophetic efforts, will often go underfunded, under-resourced and understaffed. They should not also go unimaginatively. We cannot simply stay grounded outside the door, crying out for fairness. We owe the Lord and the poor the gift of our creativity as well as our service.

One of our more creative strategies among the poor resulted in the emergence of a professional artists' guild in Los Angeles among youth who were taggers and graffiti artists. Founded in 1997, with our Los Angeles team's help, L.A. Street Productions started simple and small from the impulse of these youth. Many of these young men and women were Latinos who were not fully at home in either the Spanish-speaking world of their parents or the mainstream world of L.A.

John Tiersma Watson, a published poet and artist, recognized in the writing and freestyle tagging on walls more a restless struggle to find identity than a desire to vandalize. Some were gifted artists whose heart language, in a very real sense, was neither Spanish nor English, but art. John has a tremendous flair for improvisation in public space, and he would hang out for hours with street youth listening, challenging, befriending. He let it be known that he carried a journal that taggers and others could create in and leave their mark. Various youth, primarily young men, ranging from the taggers to disaffected youth and members of the local gang wanted to express themselves with tags, poetry and design. Some would sit for hours meditatively creating. Eventually, John realized that these young guys and girls needed a safe place beyond his apartment to gather to talk about life and the Lord, as well as draw, and he started hanging out in a place where they could again leave their mark. Magee's Donut Shop became that place, and John anchored that public space in a way that helped legitimize these youth who struggled for respect beyond the street. Everyone from heroin addicts needing their ice cream to FBI agents needing their coffee were represented at Magee's. L.A. Street Productions grew out of this creative, relational ministry and has exhibited art publicly throughout the L.A. area. They have a solid regional portfolio of clients and have secured several sizeable contracts with the City of Los Angeles to paint murals in public spaces.

Exercise Faith

Mark's account of four friends carrying the paralyzed man to Jesus is one of the great faith stories in the New Testament, and is greatly intriguing. One wonders if Mark's reference to Jesus' seeing their faith refers only to the four stretcher-carriers on the roof or includes all five men. I am confident that the paralyzed man also had faith, because I don't believe he would have let the four men tear up the roof and make a spectacle of him for no tangible return. I don't think he would risk losing his dignity when the paralysis had already taken so much.

Faith must be a critical part of ministry strategies. Faith is two-pronged. It is a means to an end and an end in itself that pleases God. In our InnerCHANGE communities, we try to resist seeing faith as simply a means to the gratifying results we all hope for. We have seen in time that much for which we have exercised faith has not come to pass exactly as we envisioned it, and we recognize that this is a common thread in biblical and Church history.

First John 5:4 reminds us, "For everyone born of God overcomes the world. This is the victory that has overcome the world, even our faith" (not our results—*our faith*). How could Abraham and so many others who obediently pursued a promise gain approval at the end of their lives with the promise only partially fulfilled? Hebrews 11 tells us they gained approval through their faith.

Performance focuses on results and is distracted into pressing for outcomes. Obedience focuses on God and bears fruit. Faith helps us distinguish the path of obedience from the drivenness of performance. I am not suggesting that we will never use terms such as "successful," "effective," "impact" or "results." I *am* saying that they cannot displace the words "faith" and "obedience" or the behaviors behind them. In a time when Western mission is numerically declining, missionaries may drive themselves more than ever into burnout conditions. One of the reasons we have organized ourselves as an order with spiritual rhythms is to help us forestall this kind of culturally inbred workaholism.

Release People into Christ's Care

One of my favorite images in this Mark 2 story is that of the four friends standing on the roof above the opening they made, watching their friend meet Jesus. These men of faith know when to obediently release their charge to the Lord. They do not climb down to the floor to carve out a further role for themselves or to worry Jesus into "doing it right." Unlike the teachers of the law grumbling among themselves about who could forgive sins, the four men on the roof knew that they could not. Only Jesus has that privilege. Their privilege was simply to help secure the meeting. In the words of John the Baptist, we need to decrease as He increases, as we go about encouraging transformation in poor communities.

Express Love

The story's final lesson for us is that of expressing love. As in "organize for action," this element, "express love," seems obvious. But in my experience of working among people who are poor, discovering and sustaining *mutual* love is not obvious—less because we are all inherently poor than because we are all inherently people. Love can be an effort.

I believe that before the four friends birthed the faith to carry this man to Jesus, they had love for him. Why do I think this? Because they did not go home when the door was crowded, and say, "Well, we tried." Instead, love compelled them to the roof. Love is often the soil that produces great faith, takes great risks. It is not said, after all, that faith lays its life down for its friend. Love is what lays its life down.

Three forces typically impel people to work among the poor. Some people are motivated primarily by mercy. Other people are drawn more to the poor out of justice. Others are driven to the poor out of guilt. They see the homeless person with little to wear and experience a rising tide of shame. They say to themselves, *Oh . . . I have so many shoes in my closet at home I don't wear.* This is only a simplistic rendering of the motives God acts on to nudge us to help "the paralyzed man."

But equally important, what will motivate us to take the man beyond the crowded door to the roof? I have often been asked, "Why do you stay working among the poor?" I stay primarily out of love. It is the growing love I have for poor people, many of whom have loved me back. It is the love and camaraderie I have experienced for my fellow stretcher-bearers. Finally, it is the growing love I have for God that He should give me the privilege to do this.

No One Talks to Each Other Here

One of my favorite stories from our ministry that illustrates this Mark 2 sequence is the orchestration of a community organization effort among Latino immigrants in the Westlake area of

Unearned Love
Abi Sutton

One evening, we had a party—time to talk, celebrate and laugh with many people from our community. The evening came to a close, but there was still cleaning up to do. I started washing dishes, and a friend of mine from the neighborhood brought back all the dishes she could find and then started drying. We weren't having a serious conversation, just chatting about our days. Out of the blue, a few minutes into our conversation, she started telling me a story about her life and how she was raised —that she was valued because she could cook and clean, and not because of who she was. I asked her if that was still how her family valued her, and she unhesitatingly said yes.

That was hard for me to hear. I have grown to value and love her not because of anything that she can do, but simply

Los Angeles. The tenants we helped were all miserably poor, many undocumented, and some unable to read and write. God enabled us to help them gain control of a 72-unit apartment complex from a "slum lord" based in Minneapolis, in the first tenant buyout and redevelopment of a private housing structure in L.A. history. In keeping with the substance of Mark 2, we took time to understand the nature of both the people and the situation, with members of our staff living in the building for several years.

A writer for the *Los Angeles Times* declared the Cambria structure "one of the worst slum disgraces in the city." Repairs had been delayed so long that the lighting had given out, toilets had

because of who she is. God delights in her and has given me a glimpse of His love for her, and it is a gift for me to share that love. Sure, there are things she does well, like seeing what needs to change, prioritizing activities and finishing tasks. But those are not the reasons she is valuable! That night, God helped me realize that as I live in this Los Angeles neighborhood, I get to share His love with others not because they "do" anything, but simply because of who they are and who they are becoming.

I was raised in a family in which I was accepted for who I am, not for what I do or accomplish. This seemed normal to me, but the older I get, the more I realize how unusual it is. My family was a safe place for me, which gave me a foundation to believe that God is a safe place—even more so than my family. Many people in my neighborhood haven't had any safe places, so they have no reason to believe that God would be any different. For them to experience His safety and unconditional love through me can give them hope that God is truly our refuge,

stopped up, and showers were broken down. A lake of sewage grew ominously in the basement. Residents began to urinate in halls and out windows. Cockroaches were everywhere and in everything, and garbage piled up in the back alley, overtaking the first-floor windows. To make matters even worse, outside the building, Cambria and Union became one of the most active corners in Los Angeles for prostitution and drug dealing.

An Uncalled Meeting

Jude Tiersma had moved into the Cambria building to sub-merge so that she could understand the conditions of the poor and share the situation as a friend. As the building deteriorated in the

Los Angeles

early 1990s, those tenants who had neither the resources nor the opportunity to move out grew desperate. Dealers and gang members began to operate openly in the Cambria building, and tenants were helpless to stop the shootings and stabbings. Finally, a group of nearly 50 residents gathered next door in the living room of InnerCHANGE members, John and Birgit Shorack. The Cambria residents had had enough, and they gathered spontaneously at the Shoracks to talk things over. They gathered there, because they had come to trust the InnerCHANGE staff and their willingness to always welcome the tenants.

That meeting in the Shoracks' home, and meetings that followed, became the seedbed for transformation. Progress was

strength and good Father. I still sometimes have a hard time believing that God uses me to show others Himself, but that is what it means to be in relationship with Him.

That night was a Kingdom intersection—the mixing of the sacred and the mundane. This friend of mine trusts me and is vulnerable with me. I can't tell you why except that God is gracious and has provided safety for both of us in this relationship. God is good, and as I choose to live among those He loves, I get to experience Him more deeply. He is present, and we can be aware of that by seeking Him. Slowly, He forms us so that we are more like Christ by giving us opportunities to love those He loves, hurt with those He hurts with, mourn with those He mourns with, and rejoice with those He rejoices with.

This is unearned, extravagant, unrelenting love. ✵

slow and halting. When Jude initially moved into the Cambria building, she was told, "No one talks to one another here." Now, residents who had never dared raise their individual voices found it even more awkward to try to forge a common voice. A gang member living in the building did all he could to impede progress. When he was shot and killed, tenants were finally able to come to agreement about proceeding with the help of Legal Aid. This agency advised the tenants to pursue legal action against the owners of the building. Through these early months, our staff resisted the temptation to take on primary roles; instead, they acted from the sidelines in encouragement. "Encouragement" may sound anemic in the face of such a mammoth undertaking as transforming a slum structure. But the power of incarnational ministry is such that when missionaries believe in poor people, poor people begin to believe in themselves.

This organizing effort proceeded slowly, seeming to travel as if in a breakdown lane. Another staff member, Paul Smith, moved into the Cambria building, partly to communicate solidarity and partly to step into a more active role in assisting three women who emerged as the most passionate leaders of the organized tenants. Paul patiently helped these three navigate the legal and political environment. God chose to use Paul Smith, a musical and math genius who orchestrated an entire student opera at Harvard, to orchestrate a level of harmony of a different magnitude among impoverished tenants.

Legal Aide helped the women—Teresa, Josefina and María—organize a legal action against the owners. The tenants won a suit in which the three landlords were charged with 42 counts of negligence. Rather than invest in costly renovation and pay stiff penalties, however, the owners hid behind a corporation and, ultimately, defaulted. It was back to the drawing board for Paul and the tenants. This was proving to be a "crowded door" experience in which the tenants could not get beyond the portal of the system. Ultimately, the restoration of Cambria took six long years. But in the process, it became a thing of beauty. Never before in L.A. had tenants become co-op owners of a building in this way. Tenants learned to be stretcher-bearers in their own interests and gained experience in improvising "on the roof." All kinds of people were creatively tapped to contribute to the success of Cambria's renovation: a USC graduate student, local officials, the mayor of Los Angeles, and the UCLA School of Architecture. Few of the people who helped were Christians, but then, God enjoys placing His Son at the head of a table of all kinds of folks.

They Must Increase

The Cambria journey is more than a story of God's glory expressed among the poor. It is a tribute to His ability to mobilize disparate hearts to help the poor and weave them into an unlikely and uncommonly beautiful fabric. The organizing project became a news item, and the tenants enjoyed their own ribbon-cutting event replete with city pomp and ceremony. Teresa, Josefina and María have been cited on several occasions with special awards, including the Community Service Award from the National Association of Organizers. They have been invited to present in Houston, Texas, and have flown to São Paolo, Brazil, to consult in a worldwide conference of organizers. São Paolo and L.A. have been pronounced sister cities as a result. One professor at UCLA continues to bring a class to the transformed Cambria building.

Neither Paul Smith nor any other InnerCHANGE staff members have been cited with any awards, nor have they sought any. They plotted out steadily decreasing roles for themselves so that the tenants could increase their roles.

The spirit of the Cambria venture is epitomized in the story of one man who took an active role in helping the effort go the distance. During the last months when contractors were finishing the building for reoccupancy, he was diagnosed with inoperable cancer. He was given two to six weeks to live. Instead, he hung on to life because he wanted to move his family back into Cambria and walk through the doors under his own power. And this he did. Two days after he moved his family into their newly renovated apartment, he left Cambria in a wheelchair and died hours later in a local hospital.

The Cambria residents who six years before had told Jude Tiersma that no one talked with each other, let alone helped each other—those same neighbors went door-to-door to take up a collection for the family of the man who died to make sure that his loved ones could stay in the building and live securely.

below the surface

They are all different; because people's needs and habits are different.
Yet they are all the same; because they have followed the same finger,
and bonded themselves by the same love.

MORRIS WEST, *THE CLOWNS OF GOD*

"I sense God calling me to mission among the poor, possibly in a place like Kazakhstan. Does it really make a difference what mission organization I go with? Can't I just find out who is already over there and join them?" We regularly field questions like this from prospective mission workers.

Does the sending body really matter? The people with whom we share our journey play a profound role in shaping who we become. Christian workers who are just starting out bond with their first mission family, and that experience, for good or ill, becomes foundational for their mission worldview.

In fact, our experience indicates that, in the early years, the community of peers one is called to minister with is more important than the initial geography one feels called to. Too often mission agencies prematurely group candidates together and launch them as teams simply because they all want to deploy to the same place, not because their gifts, skills and personal make-up complement one another. Dr. Robert Clinton, author of *The Making of a Leader*, observes that 80 percent of those who leave the mission field before their committed time is up leave due to relational issues with peers.[37] Much of this relational friction that ultimately sabotages teams becomes apparent early on as teams are forming or new people join existing teams. It can be preempted and/or prevented with deft leadership and an honest, caring community.

Choosing the right mission body can make a huge difference in sustaining oneself for the long haul. And sustaining mission workers for the long term is essential if we are to help them get to their most influential, or impact, years. Mission effectiveness, perhaps more than most careers, comes with time. Spiritual authority, so critical to seeing transformation among the poor, is something that God seems to fashion out of years of faithfulness, wise choices, successes *and* failures.

First Steps on the Journey

Regardless of how they are sent, Christian workers among the poor often begin their mission careers feeling unequal to the task. Faced with the visible scale of the need presented by most poor communities, even the most self-confident mission workers can feel intimidated. On the one hand, feelings of insufficiency in mission workers are spiritually healthy. They can act to kindle a baseline dependence on God that can translate into a life-long instinct.

On the other hand, feelings of inadequacy can spring from an insufficient self-awareness or an identity confusion and should not be simply suppressed. Insecurity deriving from these factors can deepen with time, especially if mission workers are deployed into an unstructured setting with unrealistic or unclear expectations and, furthermore, are left on their own to guide and develop themselves. Once again, Moses' story offers important insights.

God inlaid Moses life with unquestionable assets, but He also left open areas for potential woundedness. Moses' name, alone, concisely articulated his ambivalent identity. In an expression of cultural dominance, Moses' Hebrew name was wiped away when he was brought to the princess of Egypt. "She renamed him Moses, saying, 'I drew him out of the water'" (Exod. 2:10). Moses' name carried the fingerprints of God's redemptive destiny, but in the language of the oppressor. Is it any wonder that Moses required 40 years to confirm a call to mission, and that when he stepped out, he acted unwisely and acted alone?

Most of us come to mission like Moses—we are a mixed bag of assets and liabilities. The instinct of most mission entities is to push past this and quickly throw training at a new candidate with a focus on the mission *task*. Young missionaries can derive much initial self-confidence from skills-training up front. But nagging identity needs or issues relating to personal security, if allowed to go unidentified and unaddressed, eventually reveal themselves, often in negative ways in the mission field. At InnerCHANGE, we believe new mission workers benefit from having an apprenticeship in a community in which they learn skills but also learn about themselves in the context of a supportive group.

Just as important, an overemphasis on task accomplishment as the primary goal in mission, implicit or explicit, can be passed on as a value of drivenness to emerging leaders in poor communities. Most poor communities are organized relationally, and many are "villages" organized along fragile kinship lines with a high value on being, not simply doing. If task dominates our relationships with our mission authorities and peers, task will dominate our relationships with our host communities. Consequently, we will also replicate local leaders that are task-driven. We will pass on a sense of identity in doing for God rather than being in Him. In turn, these local leaders can find themselves subtly out of step with their communities. Together, we can miss an opportunity for organic expansion. Invisibly, often unwittingly, we move across the line from being missionaries among the poor to missionaries to the poor.

Big Lessons from a Little Man

Zacchaeus was a small man who likely knew what it was to feel inadequate. Insecurity about his size may have been compounded by the fact that he was a tax collector, and therefore socially despised. Luke tells us that in order to see Jesus, Zaccheus ran ahead of the crowd and climbed into a sycamore tree (see Luke 19:4). From the branches, Zacchaeus could see Jesus and, in turn, be seen by Him. This encounter with Jesus became the most important meeting of his life and directed him to the most important contribution of his life. "Look, Lord, here and now I give half of my possessions to the poor, and if I have cheated anybody out of anything, I will pay back four times the amount" (Luke 19:8). In response, Jesus told Zacchaeus that salvation had come to his house.

Certainly, this was an important tree. Without the branches to stand on, Zacchaeus was just another small man trying to peer over the crowd. Did the tree make Zacchaeus a better person? No, of course not. It simply gave him a better *position*. It raised him to a level in which he could better see Jesus and then proceed to the next step of his life.

Mission orders can act like Zacchaeus's sycamore tree and extend our work beyond where our natural abilities could otherwise take it. The support that orders give can be especially critical for those of us who humbly approach mission feeling small of stature, and direct us to meaningful contribution.

Breathing New Life into an Old Term

I believe that "order," as a word, idea and structure, is an example of a helpful tradition that needs to be re-imagined to see Kingdom mission advance sustainably among the poor.

"Order" is a powerful word that connotes mission, mystery, discipline, distinctive values and longevity. Negatively, "order" conjures images of unsmiling severity, authoritarianism, celibacy and elitism. Partly because of this mixed review and partly because orders tend to be overwhelmingly identified with the Catholic Church, Protestants, for the most part, have not formally explored orders as a vehicle for mission.

In today's world, however, I believe that the word "order" should be interpreted *structurally* rather than ideologically.

In this generation, we hold the opportunity to recapture "order" in its internal dynamics of support, not in its caricatured dynamics of restraint. In this way, a new generation of evangelical Protestants and Catholics alike can embrace a valuable tradition and reappraise and redefine it selectively for their contexts. The dictionary defines the kind of order I am discussing here as "a religious community living by mutual consent according to the principles of a common rule of life."[38] This definition affords contemporary mission leaders much latitude in forging fresh expressions of the word "order."

Discovering Our Order

Early in the formation of InnerCHANGE, we sensed God developing us as a community in ways that seemed parallel to an order. For example, we behaved more as communities than teams, apprenticed new staff in an ongoing way rather than simply training them up front, and informally made long-term commitments to one another rather than five-year plans. We came to realize that God was more intent on fashioning us as a *people*, set apart with specific values and vision, than as an organization with a job to do. Over time, we realized that we had more in common structurally with orders than with agencies. Furthermore, when we looked at the broad sweep of mission history, we found that orders proved to be durable over time—able to sustain successive waves of mission intensity spanning generations. No mission agency, for example, can claim the lifespan of the Franciscan order. From Cambodia to the Russian Steppes, everywhere we turned geographically, it appeared that the Franciscans, Dominicans or Celts had mobilized throughout history.[39]

Traditionally speaking, there are two kinds of orders: monastic orders and what I call mission orders (traditionally called mendicant orders). Monastic orders establish themselves as cloistered communities removed from the world in order to engage it through prayer and a practical model of spirituality. In a world driven by the wild horse of change, monasteries offer oases of prayer and serenity, perhaps even sanity. Monastic orders are more numerous than mission orders and tend to seize the popular imagination for what it means to be an order.

Mission orders, on the other hand, engage the world as frontline agents in the work of evangelism, church planting, teaching, and so forth. The world is their parish, and members are apprenticed as missionaries to directly advance the kingdom of God. Two of the largest and best-known mission orders are the Orders of Friars Minor (Franciscans) and the Order of Preachers (Dominicans).

Three Currents

InnerCHANGE is a mission order among the poor. Though we draw spiritual practices from the monastic orders, we engage the world head-on in the tradition of the Franciscans.

We follow a basic rule of life in upholding 10 essential values and 6 commitments. Just as important, we believe we have been raised up as a tangible expression of Micah 6:8: "He has shown you, oh man, what is good. And what does the Lord require of you? To act justly and to love mercy and to walk humbly with your God."

Proceeding from Micah 6:8, we are an order combining three essential spiritual currents in one body: the *Missionary* (love mercy), the *Prophetic* (act justly), and the *Contemplative* (walking humbly with one's God).

InnerCHANGE, then, is an order composed of communities of workers joined to God, His church, one another and the poor, commissioned as:

- **Missionaries**. In loving mercy, we are set apart as *servants* to go among the poor personally to both catalyze and assist the Church in holistic community transformation in keeping with the advancement of the kingdom of God.

- **Prophets**. In acting justly, we stand collectively as a hopeful *sign community* that seeks justice for the poor and lives a simple lifestyle that recalls the broader faith community to the upside-down aspects of Jesus' reign.

- **Contemplatives**. In walking humbly with God, we are *seekers*, exploring life-giving spiritual depth in contemplative practices and observing rhythms of prayer and community life designed to help us abide in Christ, moment by moment. We are also *stewards* of one another as God's people of inestimable value, apprenticing ourselves together in paths of personal formation that enable us to both grow as people and become more effective agents of missional transformation.

Formation Versus Training

Agencies typically train workers up front and focus on place, people group and project. As an order, we focus on the formation of our members who share a missionary call to a lifestyle of simplicity, community, service, purity, prayer and humility.

Furthermore, orders expect to be intentional about formation over a lifetime, not merely pre-field. The difference between orders and agencies is not immediately obvious, but what we have observed is that as an incarnational order among the poor, people often begin working with us because we are an incarnational ministry/mission; but they stay because we are an order.

Into the Branches of the Sycamore Tree

At the heart of who and what we are as mission orders among the poor are three key areas of support:

1. We act, reflect and sharpen one another in community, working toward a synergy of interdependent ministry efforts in which the whole is greater than the sum of its parts.

2. We seek a depth of spirituality that allows us to sustain ourselves amid the rigors and disappointments of living among the poor.

3. We seek to help our members map out an ongoing personal formation plan in the midst of a self-shaping community that ultimately draws them toward their life contribution.

We have other distinctions that mark us as an order, but these are the three essential branches of the tree that we find God using to nurture us as practitioners of justice and mercy and sustain us toward long-term service among the poor.

Crisis Around a Cup of Coffee
John Hayes

"In the 15 years I have been a missionary," said "Jerry" in a Starbucks in Manila late one night in May 2000, "I have never once had one of my leaders ask how I am doing personally and help me chart a future development plan."

I swallowed hard and wondered if Jerry, a mid-40s member of a respected international missionary agency, was exaggerating. Along with Jerry, I was sitting with Ash Barker of UNOH (Urban Neighbors of Hope) and one other friend from a missionary conference we were attending. Jerry continued, "Even when I had burned out and nearly lost both my ministry and my marriage, I had to take the initiative with my authorities. They agreed that we would return as a family to our home church in Boston for a year or so; but during that time, the organization never contacted me.

"My home church was supportive but admitted they did not have the depth of experience to counsel a dry-as-dust, middle-aged missionary. Eventually we felt whole enough to return to the Philippines. When we returned, we discovered that our new regional leader was much younger than we were and that he felt inadequate to lead us. He is a good person, but he didn't think it was fair to try to lead us. So he just turned us loose and told us to holler if we needed him."

After Jerry candidly laid out his disappointments, he asked us to tell him more about what InnerCHANGE and UNOH were doing as orders to develop our personnel. I described our efforts to provide resources and nurture our members and shared where we felt we were falling short.

Jerry's story may well be extreme in regard to the neglect of his leaders. My sense is that most missionaries are more adequately supported than he is. Nevertheless, all mission-sending entities need to renew their incentive to do their best by our workers in community growth, spirituality and personal formation. ✳

Mission Order Community

In the Gospel of Mark, Jesus promises that those who leave mothers, fathers, brothers and sisters for the sake of advancing the Kingdom will be joined to new parents, brothers and sisters on the journey. In fact, Jesus says that God will multiply them in number 100 times (see Mark 10:29-30). We believe that our InnerCHANGE communities are steps in the fulfillment of this passage. Too often mission enthusiasts stress only the first half of this passage and neglect the second. Consequently, mission workers get the impression that they are called to leave family only to be deployed alone or relatively alone in the field. Jesus knew that mission workers needed community. In the vigorous and sometimes raw work among the poor, we need a community of kindred spirits for emotional and spiritual support. An African proverb epitomizes the value of a community in one's life journey: If you want to go fast, go alone. If you want to go far, go together.

Common Commitments

Our community flows out of our primary commitments to the Lord, one another and the poor. For most of us, teammates have become some of our closest friends. However, it is important to note that the friendships did not produce the community—the community produced the friendships. Common commitments, shared values and collective purpose produced the community.

We ask new members to commit to a one-year apprenticeship. Commitment gives relationships the security they need to deepen and grow. The one-year commitment is mutual. The order commits to the apprentice just as the apprentice commits to the order. This helps release apprentices from the nagging fear that they could be just a mistake away from being asked to leave. The twelfth month of the apprenticeship is set aside as a discernment month, when both the apprentice and the community consider the next step, a two-year novitiate.

As in the apprenticeship, the novitiate concludes with a discernment period in which the novice and his/her team members prayerfully consider the next step. The next commitment period at InnerCHANGE is three years. This is followed by a sabbatical year in which we encourage the member to leave neighborhood ministry and explore other formal or informal paths of learning.

A Lesson From Gonzalo
John Shorack

I met Gonzalo on my second survey trip to Caracas in 2000, when I spent two nights sleeping on the floor of his little *ranchito* (shanty home) in the *barrio* of La Montañita. I remember sitting outside under the stars one of those nights, listening to Gonzalo, encouraging this very soft-spoken, reserved, rural man to share.

Five days after our arrival in November 2001, I visited Gonzalo in the hospital where he was recovering from a bullet wound to the stomach. That same night, in fear of the hit man's return, Gonzalo, his wife, Luisa, and their two children slipped out of the hospital. They escaped to his childhood village in the Venezuelan countryside. They returned to Caracas eight months later.

Gonzalo is a young believer. Shortly after our visit in 2000, he felt stirred to follow Christ and was baptized in a little church.

Should members decide to renew their commitments to the order after the initial seven years, they do so for seven years at a time. During every seventh year, a sabbatical is recommended for part or all of that "fallow" year. For mission workers outside the U.S., we also help set up a furlough schedule.

In general, our experience with set periods of commitment is that they liberate the member and the community to grow faster and to minister at a deeper level, much as commitment does in marriage. When one commits for a period of time and that commitment is affirmed and reflected from the community, one finds it easier to explore, to take risks and to ride out highs and lows.

Luisa, though quite timid, has been the one willing to step out and minister to her neighbors. She and two other women from the community participated for a year in a small group for discipleship and leadership training with InnerCHANGE. She co-led a home group that ministered to many needy people. She initiated after-school tutoring for children in her own community, taking in 20 children at a time under very difficult circumstances. She opened a vacation Bible club one summer, "just for the children in her immediate area." Eighty children showed up.

Three things were happening through much of this period:

1. The crime and violence by adolescent boys in La Montañita reached unbearable heights, causing great trauma and consternation on the part of many neighbors (this continues to the present).

Our staff members are both single and married. We concern ourselves with purity, not celibacy. At the same time, we encourage appreciation for both states of life, stressing the advantages of being single and those of being married. In too many mission contexts, being single is seen as an unfortunate or incomplete state, and sometimes even, singles are marginalized from leadership. This attitude is neither helpful nor biblical.

As mission workers among the poor, we seek community on several levels. We seek community with God, one another, our neighbors, the local church, Christian entities in the neighborhood with whom we may partner, sending churches, prayer

2. Luisa's co-leader in the cell group discontinued her participation, bringing an end to the cell group and its ministry in the community.
3. Gonzalo continued to sit on the sidelines, watching, evading every effort to get him to step out and minister with his wife in the community.

On one of my weekly visits to their home, I showed up with my usual ideas of what Gonzalo could do in ministry dancing in my head. *It's all about seeing God's work go forward,* I thought to myself.

"Look," I told him, "if the original plan of a cell group is too big a step, why not try doing something with sports? What do you think?"

Nothing. Gonzalo, the stoic and skeptic, wouldn't budge. Yet somehow in the midst of the conversation, one of my own teachings hit me: I'm going about this all wrong! I'm not practicing

teams, and financial supporters. All are important and add quality facets to our lives.

Community with Each Other

In InnerCHANGE, the number of times a week that a community formally gathers for prayer depends on both the mission setting and the team. Generally, we set a rhythm of regular gatherings so that we can be effective mirrors for, and ministers to, each other. Gathering together also reminds us that our synergy as the collective Body of Christ far outpaces the efficacy of ministry we might do as individuals, no matter how gifted the individual.

what I preach! It's not my job to motivate Gonzalo by pushing him to do something for God. Gonzalo doesn't need my vision and ministry ideas thrust on him. He needs a supportive person who carefully points him to God so that his experience of God becomes the springboard for whatever he steps out and does in ministry.

I don't know what God did in Gonzalo when I confessed my flawed strategy to him, but I know what happened in me. I experienced a wonderful sense of release and freedom.

Two months later, Luisa came to our house with the most interesting news. The week before, Gonzalo took four or five of the most at-risk adolescent boys of our community to the beach for an outing.

I couldn't believe my ears. "Gonzalo? Was it his idea?" "Yes," she replied. "Did he go out and invite the boys?" Again, she responded that he had. "How did it go?" I was full of excited questions. "Great," she said. "Gonzalo *even talked* with the boys." I marveled at this news, because Gonzalo is so quiet—a man of few

We must be vigilant to see one another with Kingdom eyes, always eager to help each other grow. In close proximity, we can begin to resent one another for failings, real and imagined. When we find ourselves saying that a team member "always does this" or "always says that," we can be sure that we're beginning to "know" that person into a rut, that is, project an unfair stereotype that may straitjacket personal growth. Jesus Himself encountered this several times, especially from those in and around His hometown who knew Him best. On one occasion in Capernaum, Jesus shared that He was the bread of life come down from heaven. John records that the people grumbled, saying, "Is this not Jesus, the son of Joseph, whose father and mother we know? How can

words. I celebrated that men like Gonzalo were reaching out as good neighbors to some of the violent teenage boys terrorizing our *barrio*. I also celebrated that God had used Gonzalo to help me regain perspective on my role in the community. ✳

The barrio in Caracas

he now say, 'I came down from heaven'?" (John 6:42).

At InnerCHANGE, we use various tools and exercises to help our communities remain healthy, set proper expectations for one another and flush out hidden areas of resentment that may be developing. Our teams regularly take retreats together to gain a different perspective on one another and the work, and to make space to hear God in an alternate environment.

Community with Our Neighbors

Equally important is our community with our poor neighbors. We carefully choose the homes we live in so that our staff is close enough to enjoy daily fellowship but not so close as to signal to our neighbors that we are there more for each other than for them. Our single members often live with poor families or rent homes in twos and threes in the neighborhood. We want to avoid cloistering our staff or creating a missionary compound.

We expect to learn from our neighbors and to receive from them. This is a pivotal point. In fact, let me go one step further: We expect to become dependent upon our neighbors. And we do not expect to command positions of social leverage, public or private.

Order Spirituality: Make Me Lie Down in Green Pastures

Burned-out workers produce little fruit. Transforming ministry flows from intimacy with God and a centered life. Without that intimacy, we are driven to seek identity in task, which puts our self-worth on trial for the success of that task. As Evan Howard says, we need a spirituality that does not merely arrange the chaotic edges of our lives but rises from and finds the very center of our lives.[40]

Mission workers among the poor need a contemplative spirituality. We can be notorious doers. At the heart of being contemplative is abiding in Christ. The contemplative life helps to keep us replenished and centered when the pressures of mission life stretch us beyond all recognition.

If we cannot allow ourselves to be tired from the mission ministry, we will get tired *of* the ministry. As good Samaritans on the road crowded with the needy, the guilt of not doing enough can worm away our resolve from the inside. The stress of living in neighborhoods that often run over our personal boundaries and violate our

A Late Night Chat with My Dog
Darren Prince

It was late in the evening—close to 11:00 P.M. I was on a run with my dog, Peanut, up Bernal Hill. The cold night air was crisp and so clear that I could see all the lights of San Francisco in the valleys below me.

I reached the part of my run where the pain of getting started gave way to an energizing sense of warmth. My breathing was deep. My cheeks were burning. My mind was clear. I turned and said to Peanut, "This feels so good . . . why didn't I ever do this when I was in the thick of ministry?"

Almost as soon as I finished asking Peanut the question, she "answered" it.

"You never had time to do this because you were busy with ministry."

needs for space and quiet can overwhelm us from the outside. As we feel our emotional resources draining, the instinct is to step backward toward a smaller, safer life. Instead, in embracing a contemplative spirituality, we step forward toward a bigger, abler God. He is likely to direct us to downsize our lives or move toward a closer coworking with others. In the press of the work itself, to abide in Christ means to reprogram our instincts to step first toward the unseen God. Stepping toward God in mystical union with Him is also a step toward our brothers and sisters in the neighborhood.

In my own life, I have found this easier said than done. I am not a natural contemplative who instinctively abides in Christ. Often, when I read in the news about a crisis or tragedy, I am

My newly cleared mind would not accept this response, so a casual (and imaginary) dialogue with Peanut began:

"But this is exactly what my mind and body needed to cope with ministry stress. Exercise like this would have been so good for me."

"You're right. But you were so busy doing ministry that you didn't do any of the very life-giving things that would have sustained you."

"Isn't that what incarnational ministry is all about? Your ministry is your life?"

"That's how you've been doing it for six years! In fact, the opposite is true: Your ministry is not your life; your life should be your ministry."

"What's the difference?"

"It's a tiny change in word order, but there's a gigantic difference—one that will lead you to burnout and misery if you confuse the two."

quicker with an opinion or action plan than I am to pray. I take encouragement when I recall the disciples' record in prayer, especially Peter's.

At Jesus' transfiguration, when Jesus chose Peter, James and John to accompany Him, Luke tells us that they ascended a mountain to pray (see Luke 9:28-36). As seems to have happened on other occasions when prayer was Jesus' agenda, the disciples fell asleep—after all, there was nothing to *do*. However, when Moses and Elijah appear on the mountain and, with Christ, are transformed into heavenly splendor, the disciples awakened. It's curious that the disciples' first reaction seems not to have been prayerful awe. In fact, Peter reacted by suggesting a project. He

"Go on."

"When ministry is your life, you will give when you have nothing to give, work when you should be resting, neglect that which should be your greatest priority, and ultimately loathe the very people you are called to love. In short, when ministry is your life, you have no life to offer to others and nothing but ministry to invite others into."

"Sounds like me," I reply.

"On the other hand, when your life is your ministry, all of life becomes a sacrament before God: your work and your rest, your eating and sleeping, your generosity and your neediness, your care for your body and the environment, your trivial pastimes and your greatest accomplishments. When all of your life is what you offer as your ministry, then nothing is wasted. In short, when your life is what you offer to others as ministry, what you offer is multifaceted and rich with meaning."

suggested that they build three booths to honor Jesus and the two prophets.

God sent down a cloud to envelop the disciples. Wrapped in this holy fog, they could no longer see clearly enough to do anything; they could only *be* present to the Lord and listen. God spoke and told them who Jesus is and admonished them to listen to Him. This story reminds me that there are times when God wants to separate us from our physical capabilities and impulses to act and enclose us in a contemplative posture that liberates our spiritual capacities.

One way to tangibly step toward God is to establish a rhythm of taking spiritual retreats. Most missionaries among the poor

"Are you suggesting that going for a run with my dog is just as significant as any of my ministry objectives?"

"Not only is it significant, but it is also vital. Without a fully lived life, what you present to God and to others is one-dimensional and incomplete. The lost are compelled to follow Christ when they see how you do life—how you treat your children, where you buy your groceries, how you care for your neighbors—not by how much you do ministry."

"So all those times when I skipped lunch and pulled all-nighters for the sake of the ministry—"

"The people you were discipling saw a man living a life of destruction."

"Then what did people learn from me?"

"How to live an unbalanced, chaotic life of ministry that ruins the soul rather than nourishes it."

"And if I had dropped what seemed so important to go for a run or to cook lunch?"

find this difficult to do. Either we feel guilty taking a retreat away from needy neighbors or we feel unequal to the task of planing far enough ahead to take one. Consequently, retreats become occasional episodes of collapse rather than rhythms of refuge and regeneration. Rob Yackley, founder of Nieu Communities, points out that Psalm 23:2 states, "He *makes* me lie down in green pastures" (emphasis added).[41] At InnerCHANGE, we try to be vigilant on one another's behalf to see that retreats and other life-giving exercises are followed.

Aside from taking retreats, we can facilitate the process of stepping toward God in all things by pursuing spiritual disciplines. These include keeping the Sabbath and daily times with

"Your followers would have seen a man unapologetically living the kind of abundant life Jesus calls us to."

I want that kind of abundance. I want that kind of life. My ministry is not my life, but my life can be my ministry. ✳

Peanut

the Lord, not simply in Bible study but also in continually feeding on God's presence. Journaling, guided reflection, meditation and fasting can also be helpful. Many of our members use the Ignatian exercises for certain seasons or seek an outside spiritual director. We have discovered that discipline takes us toward a more light-footed spirituality. In the same way that discipline allows a ballet dancer or gymnast to soar effortlessly, "discipline for the purposes of godliness" (1 Tim. 4:7) gives wings to our spiritual life.

Contemplative spirituality does not simply come naturally, especially in a ministry as active as that of working among the poor. We must make space for it, as individuals and as teams. Meeting God cannot be optional or pushed to the times "when we need it." Among the poor, our spirituality must also include a biblical theology of suffering. We must allow disappointment to drive us to the constant company of God and out of our theological paper houses and the shallow comfort of "answers." With so many unreached poor and so few Christian workers who will live among them, it is easy to feel as though we ourselves are the mere 5 loaves and 2 fish in the face of 5,000 hungry people. Contemplative spirituality encourages us to believe that God will multiply our lives as He sees fit. We must also cultivate a theology of celebration, personally experiencing the joy of being with the Bridegroom.

substance building

There are qualities of life that are merely a choice away.

JOHN TIERSMA WATSON

In the early 1980s, Los Angeles epitomized the modern world-class city of two faces: one with a bright neon smile and another with a gray, toothless grimace. During my two years directing the L.A. STEP Foundation, I found myself exploring the broken-down streets near that world-class city's downtown district, just north of the area called South Central.

In my work, I met two lay ministers I will call Jim and Rob, working the streets from their base at the Union Rescue Mission. Both had done time, been homeless and met Christ at the Union Rescue Mission. Jim had discovered that single rooms in flophouse hotels overlooking Skid Row were homes to entire Latino families. Most had come across the border illegally. The conditions inside these dark hotels were as bad as any I have seen in the two-thirds world. There were only single bathrooms down shattered halls, doors ripped off hinges like empty eye sockets, and toilet seats stripped away. Jim and Rob, along with a committed group of volunteers, had started to give donated food to these families, and I joined in the effort.

As our efforts gathered momentum, Jim wanted to go beyond securing food donations from church pantries and city food banks and build a broader resource base. Jim and Rob asked me to act as chairman of the board of what was meant to be a formal organization, one that could raise funds, while Jim served as executive director. I agreed to take on this role because it seemed so compatible with STEP goals, and it allowed me to walk "turf" beyond South Central.

Some time passed, and Jim informed me that he could not account for several thousand dollars donated from the United Way, funds purportedly promised to a community center in South Central. Then, Jim disappeared. Several days later, he called me, distraught, from a hotel in Phoenix. He said he had taken no money, and I believe he was telling the truth. But the executive director of the community center promised to take legal action to redress the matter, and Jim was fearful of facing charges again. "I can't go back, John," he said. "I just can't go back to prison." I did not press him. After talking with him, I left a message with my friend Jerry Turner, a top-flight lawyer I had met at church.

When Jerry phoned me back, he quickly got my attention. He told me that as chairman of the board of a formal entity, it could be construed that I had "a duty to know" the financial state of affairs Jim had presided over. I'll never forget the dull thud of alarm I felt as Jerry spelled out the hazards I faced alone in Jim's absence. By this time, Rob was also nowhere to be found. Still, I resisted the instinct to look for Jim and Rob. Instead, I asked Jerry if he could come to South Central that Monday morning and join me in meeting with Dr. E. V. Hill, my pastor and supervisor for my work with the STEP Foundation.

I remember sticking uncomfortably to the leather of Jerry's vintage Porsche as we drove to Mount Zion Missionary Baptist Church. Jerry brought Dr. Hill up to speed. My pastor leaned back as he listened patiently, recognizing in my quandary the potential implications for Mount Zion's substantial ministries in South Central and his personal reputation in the city. As I listened to Jerry, I began to wonder if I might get fired. In a sentence I'll never forget, Dr. Hill graciously affirmed me and

The Voice of God on the Street
Nate Bacon

It was a bright sunny morning, around 10:00 A.M., in San Francisco's Mission District. I stood in front of our apartment building on 24th Street, observing the movements around me. In the tiny city park next to our building, there were four young men dressed in clothes typical of the local gangs. They were tagging (spray-painting their gang logos and street names) on some of the park benches.

When they realized that I was watching them, they yelled out, "What are you looking at?" I calmly responded that I was just watching them. "Well, turn around and keep walking!" came the clipped response.

The wise thing to do would have been to keep walking and avoid any further problems, but inside of me, I sensed that God

my learning curve in L.A. He said, "Well, John got his bachelor's degree at Princeton, his master's at Yale, and now he's getting his Ph.D. on the streets." He counseled Jerry and me in approaching the director of the community center who was threatening the lawsuit.

In the end, the case against our fledgling entity providing food for needy families was dropped. Sadly, I closed down our operation and never saw Jim or Rob again. But I walked away from that meeting with Dr. Hill convinced of a quality of knowledge available on the streets—and only experience could gain it. Years later, in InnerCHANGE, we began to call this "action/reflection" learning, or "Seminary in the Streets."

wanted me to stay there. When they realized that I had not moved, they rushed toward me to confront me, and one of them got literally in my face. A conversation of sorts ensued in which, internally, I was continuing to question God—did He really want me to stay there? As calm as I was trying to be externally, I noticed with growing alarm that the young man confronting me had taken off his jacket. He told me that I had three seconds to "turn around and keep walking!"

"God, is that You, really?" I cried out internally. I continued to feel that God wanted me to stay where I was. In that very instant, another of the young men blurted, "It's 'cause you didn't show us respect!"

Thanks be to God, this intervention began to change the tone of the conversation by giving substance to our standoff. I assured them that it was not my intention to show lack of respect, and I apologized. However, I also asserted that they had disrespected me, as well, that I lived there and had a right to look around where I wanted.

Being part of an order means taking an enhanced view of personal formation. We must not allow ourselves to slide into a daily frenzy of activity that crowds out any thought of future development, or we deny not only ourselves but also our communities. Unless a person keeps an eye to the future, it's easy to stray from the path. Only when we watch the road far ahead can we steer a straight course. In this we have been profoundly shaped by long-time friend Dr. Bobby Clinton, who contends that maintaining a lifetime perspective and being a lifelong learner are essential to finishing well.

When Jesus looked at Zacchaeus, He did not say, "By the way, it's too bad you're not taller." Nor did Christ step forward and

As things calmed down further, we began to talk, and I said that I worked with the church. The one who had been most confrontational responded, "I don't believe in God!" Almost simultaneously, the young man who had intervened responded, "I go to St. Anthony's!" When they further discovered that we visited inmates of juvenile hall (we had begun doing so only a few months earlier) the tone changed further, and the very guy who had wanted to jump me said, "Maybe you can help me."

God worked in the life of that young man and continued to give us opportunities to see each other. He ended up going to college and believing in God, and has overcome many painful childhood moments.

A couple of years later, I ran into him on the street and he told me that he had just been talking to his girlfriend about me. He was explaining to her how a voice inside him that day had told him not to hit me, and how he has learned to pay attention to that voice. I realized in that moment that we had both heard the same voice and learned identical lessons that day at the park. ✳

supernaturally raise Zacchaeus's stature. In the same way, developing a person is not merely about remedying his or her individual deficiencies. Raising competencies to address shortcomings is a key component of skills training. But *forming* people looks both to the individual and to the community, considering every person as they fit into the Body of Christ. One person's weakness is invitation to another's strength. All are not apostles, are they? All are not prophets, are they? All do not have the gift of healing, do they? (See 1 Cor. 12:29-30.)

We strive toward complementary ministries in InnerCHANGE that interlock. Consequently, we assume that our members' spiritual gifts, natural abilities and acquired skills will interlock as well. In our development of people, we not only begin by training in core competencies for ministry among the poor, but we also help an apprentice make a careful self-assessment. We use several tools to stimulate this self-awareness, including artistically rendered personal timelines, the Meyers-Briggs personality indicators, spiritual gift discovery, and something we call "The Big Rocks Exercise." The better we know ourselves, the better we know how we fit together in community and can complement one another.

A second reason we begin immediately to help apprentices, even interns, get in touch with who they are and what they bring to a community is because we want to alert them quickly to the importance of character. Ultimately, lasting ministry flows more from our being, or who we are, than from what we can do. Character takes a lifetime to develop; skills do not. Mission formation is more than developing a skill.

This is not to say we do not have intentional tracks for ongoing skill development. We do have these, and many are very sophisticated; but in general, they are integrated holistically with spiritual and character formation. The axis for our skill formation is action/reflection bathed in prayer. In this effort, a Chinese proverb inspires us: I hear, I forget. I see, I remember. I do, I understand. Our bias is to help our members value and understand their own experience and measure it against that of others. We do very little in the classroom. We steer toward action/reflection partly because we have found it a more appropriate learning style for our context. Ministry is at least as much art as science. It is largely the profound art of making relationships. Art is often learned better in an action/reflection mode than in an academic setting. The second reason we rely so heavily on an action/reflec-

A View from the Wall

John Green, Emmaus Ministries, Chicago

On this night, I'm holding up a wall. My back presses flat against the coarse brick. I bend my right knee, with the sole of my foot against the wall behind me. It's a good wall to lean against.

I'm a silent sentry on Hubbard Street. From my sentry post, I can see about a dozen guys, hustling, and about two-dozen "johns" (customers) cruising in their cars.

One john eyes me up and down as he slowly passes by. I laugh; he's not going to get a "date" out of me. I recognize some of the johns from the few years I've been coming down here. Some turn their heads away when they see me, their guilt getting the best of them.

They make me angry, these predators. The hustlers I pray for have chosen to do this kind of work to put food in their mouths or to support a family, although some do it more to support a drug

tion model is that it is a style the poor themselves can quickly master. It makes sense to develop our people with methods they can then use among the poor.

Formation is one of the most critical factors affecting the Christian worker's impact over a lifetime, and focuses as much on the little things we do as disciples as on our larger hopes and dreams. It is often in the context of a community of other committed disciples of Jesus that we find we can be guided and asked the tough questions that shape us as people.

Gerald Arbuckle describes this process in *Out of Chaos: Refounding Religious Congregations:*

habit now. For most of them, prostitution first began as a way to survive.

Many of the johns are older white males from the 'burbs. Some are driving cars that are about five years' worth of salary for me. Some have baby-carrier car seats in the back, a silent testimony to the wife and family who are oblivious to Daddy's midnight jaunts.

It's not a nice world I see from my wall.

Catercorner from my post, Tim is making a fool of himself, yelling and laughing. He's one of those guys who's always up— always has a smile—even when he's trying to sell himself. He screams a hello and jaywalks across to me. I tell him to be careful—he might get arrested that way. We laugh. He's talking to me, but his eyes are on the street, watching the passing predators for any sign of interest.

A john, or "date" as some of the guys call them, pulls up and Tim gets in.

Formation for prophetic mission is a process whereby a person in and through community assumes responsibility for his/her growth in Christ, in the service of the church and society, according to the founding experience of his/her particular congregation. It is a process of liberation by which, under skilled guides, a person frees himself/herself from constraints of: a personal order (sin, pride, ignorance of Christ as the center of life, ignorance of academic/pastoral skills necessary to be part of Christ's mission today); and a social or cultural order (undue cultural pressures, prejudices).[42]

"Be back in a few," he says. His smile disappears.

Around the corner comes Randy. Five rehab tries and still counting—he remains a major cokehead. Youth and a strong heart might see him through it.

He's surprised that I don't give him one of my usual lectures. I'm all lectured out, I say. I tell him that I will pray that the next time I see him isn't on a slab at the morgue. He walks away in silence.

When Anthony comes around the corner with a new guy named Mike, the new guy eyes me suspiciously. Anthony assures him that I'm not a cop and goes on to tell him about the camping trip I took him and three other hustlers on last year. Mike introduces himself and takes one of my cards. I explain the ministry a bit.

Anthony and Tim, who is back from his "date," are trying to decide whether or not to go with a john they don't know down to 84th street on the south side. He's willing to pay $300.

Three Stages of the Journey

One of the legacies of the "real world" mind-set of today, especially in the West, is the concept of the bottom line. Consequently, an implicit scale of measure that throws outcomes into just two categories—successes and failures—haunts our efforts. There is no credit for trying hard. The result of this bottom-line thinking is that we are wooed away from Kingdom obedience into performing for success. As members of orders, we are not immune from this cultural influence. This is yet another reason we invest so heavily in maintaining healthy community, mining deep veins of spirituality, and encouraging one another to grow. One tangible expression of our

The john has been trying to pick someone up all night. The guys are leery of new people. Jeffrey Dahmer and John Wayne Gacy were both "new people" when they cruised this block. That's one of the real dangers guys like Anthony and Tim face. They make easy targets for killers and crazies.

Anthony needs the cash, so he gets in the car on its next lap around the corner. And I say a silent prayer.

Mike has been talking to me about his growing up in the church. We talk about God, Jesus, sin, forgiveness. Mike is a bit of a theologian. His mom, he says, told him that God wants us to be happy.

God does not promise us that we will be happy, I say, but He does promise us joy. As a Christian, you can be joyful even in the midst of pain and struggle.

Mike smiles and says he understands. He has to get back to business and shakes my hand. Be joyful, I say.

It's been three hours; my sentry time is done. I leave my post and begin to walk toward my car to head uptown to another strip.

spirituality is the concept of journey. We describe ourselves as "journey people," that is, we are alert to see ourselves from a long-term perspective, not simply in the present. This contemplative posture encourages us to reflect on the road behind and the way ahead and helps lift us out of the frenzy to perform today.

The experience of the Exodus alternative community is an especially instructive paradigm for mission communities journeying among the poor. The Israelites passed through three distinct stages: *the ideal*—deliverance from Egypt; *the ordeal*—time in the desert or wilderness; and *the new deal*—destiny, the Promised Land. (Pastor Tim Timmons used these terms to refer to the successive stages of a marriage.)

And I say a prayer.

Watch over my guys, Lord; keep them safe. May I, and our other street ministers, bring some light and hope to this sad world. ✳

Chicago

For the Israelites, the ideal process began with the first plague and reached its pinnacle on the far bank of the Red Sea as God's people watched the waters bury their enemies. That victory seemed to confirm for a small nation their break with the Egyptian empire, the power of the world at that time.

Most of our members experience a similar ideal phase in first coming into a poor community in the company of like-minded coworkers. We feel liberated from the "real world" and its drive to get ahead and we find new purpose in working for eternal results among the most needy. For a few of us, the danger and risk of ministering on the street adds a glamour that contributes to the ideal.

Eventually, the ideal gives way to the ordeal. Typically, the ordeal comes to us in the form of unmet expectations and culture shock. Along the way, we become disappointed that God hasn't performed more miracles on behalf of the poor, or that our own growth seems to proceed at a snail's pace, or that our coworkers are not quite the spiritual giants they seemed to be at first. And of course, the poor don't seem to appreciate us as much as we thought they would and they are not quite as captivated by our visions of transformation as we are.

Unfortunately, the ordeal is a season during which many Christian workers among the poor burn out and/or check out. In fact, many enter the work knowing instinctively that burnout is an "honorable discharge" from the ministry. The Protestant mainstream has come to expect that incarnational mission workers among the poor will encounter the ordeal and leave, and this helps to confirm the pattern. This is where the Catholic orders, with their ability to sustain workers among the poor for lifetimes of service, are so instructive. They encourage us to see the ordeal through a new lens and respond to it in a different way.

The Desert—More Than Hot Sand

When God fashions for Himself a new people, He does it in the context of adversity. God uses the *ordeal* phase to confirm the new identity established in the *ideal* period. As if it were not traumatic enough to break with the mainstream and be turned upside-down, God gives us the desert to cross. The break with Egypt was not the end of the journey, but the beginning.

Some of us never anticipated the desert, or if we did, we thought of it as a distance to cover as quickly as possible. We didn't necessarily think of it as a character journey, a way for God to take our commitments to service and confirm them as our lives, not just as our dreams. The desert, it turns out, is more than a place with hot sand.

Throughout Scripture, God draws people together into alternative communities and releases them into *ordeals*. When Nehemiah led a remnant back to Jerusalem to rebuild the wall, the Israelites had to rebuild the wall in the teeth of their enemies, one hand laying bricks, the other hand on their swords. Similarly, the new Church recorded in Acts is a story recorded in blood. Stephen, Paul and nearly all of the first leaders of the Church paid for their commitment with their lives.

Why the desert? Why the difficulty? It is difficult to see purpose in the ordeal stage of the journey—banded together, under-resourced in finances, struggling to grow our teams, struggling with conflict internally, weary of explaining ourselves to an intimidated or guilt-ridden mainstream Church, tired of scanning the horizon line for a glimpse of the promised land.

Why the desert? A primary reason is that God wants His people to march opposite *to* the world in order to establish them as a counterculture *in* the world. The only way to confirm that counterculture is to create it in adversity. God is concerned for our spiritual survivability, but He is also concerned that our prophetic voice should not become domesticated over time.

The long journey across the desert is His way of starving out our last attitudes from Egypt, or in some cases, the hangover of a consumer Christianity. He tests us in the desert to see if we will sacrifice our new freedom for security. The ordeal is really the process of hammering our ideal into His ideal.

So when we pass from the ordeal into the new deal (into the promised land), will the struggle cease? In the Exodus story, the Israelites had to fight for their land inch by inch (see Exod. 23:29-30). Perhaps there will be a time in missional communities when there is a critical mass of staff, when budgets increase, and when indigenous leaders arrive in greater numbers.

However, we never perfectly or completely arrive. The new deal brings new struggles. But being small, or unfinished, does not imply being unimportant. "The LORD did not set his affection on you and choose you because you were more numerous than other peoples, for you were the fewest of all peoples. But it was because the LORD loved you" (Deut. 7:7).

The Journey Is the Destination

In our journey, as in the Exodus journey, God establishes that abiding in His presence is the goal, rather than arriving at a geographical—or even a heavenly—location. It is human nature to focus on the tangible promised land, to see God as a means to the end. But as a Christian order among the poor, we need to remember that Jesus is the way, not just the One who shows the way. Moses understood well the need for God's constant company and how that presence set the Hebrews apart as a people: "If your presence will not go, do not carry us up from here. For how shall it be known that I have found favor in your sight, I and your people, unless you go with us? In this way, we shall be distinct, I and your people, from every people on the face of the earth" (Exod. 33:14-16).

When God fashions a community for Himself, its values and patterns matter down to the smallest detail. God shows us this with Leviticus and Deuteronomy, in which He fleshes out in micro-fashion the macro-vision of being a new people in a new land. In other words, new orders can expect a season of complexity as new frameworks emerge for incarnational ministry aimed at bringing others into the extended family of the community of faith.

Collective Memory
"When we lose our memory, we lose our way" is an InnerCHANGE paraphrase of an African proverb. The journey through the ordeal forms and confirms new identity and prioritizes God's company over the destination. It also forges collective memory, or corporate history. On the eve of the crossing over the Jordan into the Promised Land, God instructed Moses to deliver a final charge to the people. This is recorded for us in the book of Deuteronomy. In those 34 chapters, Moses used the commands "Remember" or "Do not for-

get" 24 times. It was God's intention that the people enter their new land with their history of the journey as a treasure and a cultural safeguard. Corporate history remembered in a living way can also spur us to continue to faithfully step forward. David, the shepherd boy, went out to face Goliath without a special word from the Lord that he would triumph. Instead, he was compelled forward with a vigilant memory of how God had caused him to conquer the bear and the lion (see 1 Sam. 17:34-35). Similarly, collective memory became the motivating force of the Hebrews in a hostile land.

Orders, when they nurture their histories, offer this testimony of God's faithfulness to new generations of members as a dowry. Alternatively, when we follow the corporate model of simply giving a thumbnail sketch of organizational history at orientation, we miss the opportunity to arm new members with an inspirational past to proceed from. In InnerCHANGE, we have been challenged by God's record in Deuteronomy to cultivate active remembrance of our history. To accomplish this, we intentionally share stories informally and formally, celebrate our history when we gather, and use our stories as primary case studies in developing formation materials.

We also work hard to nurture our understanding and appreciation of Church history. This means reaching past the birth of the Protestant Reformation to draw inspiration from traditionally Catholic influences: the wisdom of the desert fathers and the prophetic simplicity of the Franciscans, for example. Our Catholic members in InnerCHANGE are a living reminder that those of us who are more comfortable in the Protestant traditions neglect the richness of the Church's collective history at our own peril. While we raise eyebrows in some circles by naming our ecumenism for what it is, we find that we are better torch-bearers for collective memory when we draw on the best of all of our traditions.

The broader scope of Church history, combined with our own collective history as InnerCHANGE, helps our new members grow faster and start surer than we did as the pioneers. Insights from our past help us interpret our present and shape our future expectations for this journey as an order among the poor. In turn, this encourages us to advance and keeps us from shrinking back in longing for the comforts, security and certainty of Egypt.

Artistry for the Journey

God saves His most detailed instructions to the Israelites for the commissioning of the traveling tabernacle. Smack in the middle of a grueling journey through the desert, God asks His people to pour their artistic treasure and talents into the making of a movable home in which He can dwell. This isn't God playing the part of general manager, making sure His people have enough to occupy their time on their way to the Promised Land. Nor is it God playing interior decorator for the sake of whimsy. In the midst of a massive movement of His people, He commissions them to be artists along the way: capturing the grandeur of God and retelling their stories in symbol and imagery.

Originally, we were puzzled with the number of artists God seemed to be bringing into our midst. Skilled and talented poets, musicians, photographers and painters have all found their home within the family of InnerCHANGE. Why such a high rate of artistically motivated people in a missional order serving among the poor? Perhaps because the journey from ideal through ordeal is best interpreted through the eyes, ears and fingertips of collective artistry. Perhaps because God seems to form His people by forming the whole person: the right brain in concert with the left, the artists and engineers working together. InnerCHANGE's manifest, like the Israelites', isn't just to get from point A to point B, but to create something beautiful along the way. In the process, we become something beautiful as well.

Laila (right) in Caracas

CHAPTER 10

water pressure

The ship is safest when it is in port. But that's not what ships were made for.

PAULO COEHLO

I remember March 1, 1993, with vivid clarity. It was the second to last day Deanna and I were in Cambodia on a two-month exploratory trip to scout Phnom Penh as a potential ministry site. We were living in a two-room cement block apartment with an elderly woman named Ohm Sokhum and her adopted daughter, Naat. Prior to the Khmer Rouge takeover in 1975, the space had most likely been a storefront; there were no windows in front, just a sliding metal curtain. At night, Ohm closed the metal gate for security, and the heat would build inside, unrelieved by airflow. Consequently, Ohm would leave the sliding curtain open as long as she felt it was safe to do so.

That evening, the sliding gate was still partly open, and the slanting rays of the sun settled in a warm band on the left wall. Ohm was sitting on the platform next to the front opening, her face catching the amber light in a way reminiscent of renaissance portraiture. Next to her sat Naat, 12 years old, but looking younger. Deanna and I were sitting in the center of the front room on the double bed of wooden slats, our journals and Bibles out as we reflected on our stay in Cambodia.

Ohm and Naat had made dinner, taking care to include all of our favorite foods. I was well beyond comfortably stuffed, and I kept glancing at Ohm and Naat affectionately. Naat contentedly swung her legs off the edge of the platform. Ohm looked wistful as she sat perfectly still, listening to the motos and the foot-pedaled taxis, called "cyclos," slip by on Tuosamouth Boulevard. In our time together, we had come to call her mother. Ohm's three children, her husband and most of her extended family were murdered in 1975 when the Khmer Rouge overran the city. Her oldest son would have been exactly my age, 38, had he survived.

Suddenly the door was yanked open with a shrill scraping sound. Pastor Kakedaa nodded respectfully to Ohm and stepped into the room. He began to fire phrases in machine-gun fashion, overwhelming my moderate fluency. Eventually, we understood that Kakedaa wanted us to follow him to pray for a woman who was gravely sick, possibly dying.

Deanna and I instinctively react out of mercy in situations like these. However, because this was Cambodia in the 1990s, a country that paid disproportionate deference to Westerners, we also were careful to discern up front if this was an opportunity to empower a local leader. Deanna and I asked Pastor Kakedaa if he had already prayed for this woman.

"Many times," Kakedaa informed us. He told us the woman had been sick a very long time, and Kakedaa had drawn in local pastors and Western visitors to pray for healing for her. Deanna and I agreed to go. Kakedaa threaded us into traffic on his motorbike and then wound through a number of narrow side streets as the sun slid behind the buildings. Finally, Kakedaa parked in front of one of the tallest buildings I'd seen in Phnom Penh—at least four floors, maybe five. Its unfinished exterior, with dark cavities, gave it the appearance of a parking garage. We stepped into an enclosed stairwell. As we climbed the stairs behind Kakedaa, I noticed dark stains on the wall, and deep gouge marks where metal bolts had been torn out. I wondered if Pol Pot's Communists had used this solid structure as a holding facility to torture resistant Khmer.[43]

At the top floor, we entered a doorless room. The room was bare and hushed in shadow. In the left-hand corner, I made out the bright red features of a Buddhist wall shrine. The air in the room was so still the smoke from the incense burned straight upward. Only as our movement disturbed the room did the gray line begin to spiral slightly. As my eyes adjusted, I noticed that there was a doorway at the back of the room, and a slender man was standing in it. Kakedaa politely greeted the man but there was no warmth in the exchange. Pastor Kakedaa whispered in limited English that the man was a strong Buddhist. Almost directly underfoot, a skeletal woman lay on a pallet. Her body was so wasted with disease that I doubt she weighed more than 50 pounds. The skin on her face was pulled so tight that her mouth was stretched into part grimace, part smile. As she watched us, her head began to turn back and forth with the precision of a metronome. I sank to my knees next to her as Deanna gently took the woman's hand. I was gripped with a sadness so sudden and deep that I felt as if my emotions had dropped down an elevator shaft. Deanna and I exchanged glances, both of us determined to pray for her and release the outcome to God. We asked Kakedaa to join us, and he knelt beside us.

Prayer mentors had taught us to dignify people as Christ so often had by asking them how they wanted to be prayed for. The woman could not speak, so Kakedaa asked the man behind us on her behalf. We learned that this man was her husband. Her exact medical condition got lost in translation, but her husband confirmed that she had seen several doctors and received many visitors who had prayed for her. Deanna and I sensed that the woman was experiencing demonic oppression in addition to disease. At moments, her eyes were desperately alive in a body that was a prison. I wondered how a woman could survive this abiding trauma, as day tailgated day in seamless sameness.

We spent some time quietly listening together for God's voice. When we sensed His affirmation, we proceeded to pray for this woman, both silently and aloud, for what felt like a long time. All the while, we held her hands, stroked her arms and face. Kakedaa seemed to catch fire and prayed with great passion. Slowly the woman's head stopped turning, and her eyes expressed gratitude. The fact that we spoke to her in Cambodian seemed to endear us to her, and I felt that she especially connected with Deanna. Who was this young blonde woman, so other, who touched and spoke with such compassion? The tension in the room seemed to lift. The woman's husband relaxed and sat behind us on a low couch. The husband chatted a bit now, warmly even, eager to find out more about us and our stay in Cambodia.

But it was clear this woman was not about to rise and walk. Kakedaa seemed not to be surprised or even especially disappointed. This man had seen terrors in the 1970s that I could only guess at. We said good-bye, climbed back down the stairs and lingered outside for a moment. I could tell that Kakedaa was grateful we had come. I told Kakedaa that I believed God would do what God would do, and that occasionally in our experience, God brought healing or a measure of relief overnight. Since Kakedaa was to pick us up in the morning to take us to the airport, I asked him if he could stop by this woman's apartment on the way and determine if she had experienced any change. We all agreed that God had given us the privilege to pray and that we would continue to pray for this woman.

Kakedaa asked if he could drive us back to Ohm's on his bike, but I needed a respite to reflect before we rejoined Ohm, so we decided to walk back. Deanna and I were emotionally rung out, and we didn't talk much on the walk back to Ohm's. Both of us were still experiencing the shadow of a deep-in-the-soul sorrow.

That final night with Ohm was poignant. We all stayed up late talking, promising to write and to pray for one another. (We found out the next time we were in Cambodia that Ohm prayed for us daily, often as many as three times a day.)

That night I could not sleep at all because I kept turning over in my mind our encounter with the woman immobilized by disease. Staring into the mosquito net, I'd see her face and experience a fresh rush of emotion. I would close my eyes and try to sleep, but her infrared after-image remained. Finally, I sat up and came face to face with my disappointment.

I poured out my emotions to the Lord. I had seen Him work in that room in the small things: the peace the woman seemed to gain as we prayed, the cultivation of the husband's appreciation, the experience of tangibly being the Body of Christ with Kakedaa. I tried to be satisfied with this, but when I thought of the woman's pain, the darkness in that room that was like a cellblock, I just could not understand how healing this desperately stricken woman could be anything other than good news. Good news for her. Good news for her family. Healing her body would tangibly express God's love and act as a sign of God's authority to a family that so obviously could benefit from a powerful faith builder.

The next morning, Kakedaa and numbers of other friends descended on Ohm's house for final good-byes. We were ushered to the airport by a crowd, some riding motos, others in cyclos, and Ohm, Naat, Deanna and me in an arthritic Russian sedan. In the flurry, I asked Kakedaa if he'd been able to check on the woman we had prayed for the night before. He hadn't seen the woman.

Waiting, the Quiet Assassin

We boarded the plane, arrived in Southern California, and returned to our Cambodian complex in Long Beach. As we regained our routine in the community, I thought less and less about the woman in Cambodia. I continued to pray for her, as did my wife, but in my heart, I suspected she had died, and I had already turned to grieving. Yet, in the back of my mind, I was still waiting for a final word from Kakedaa. About six weeks after coming home, we received a letter from Phnom Penh. Kakedaa's Cambodian writing was hard to follow, so Deanna read me the letter. It was full of good news on the local church scene, and we were gratified. It closed with a terse sentence saying, "The old woman died."

In the months that followed our trip to Cambodia, I found myself slipping emotionally. Insomnia, a lifelong problem, intensified. Days slipped by in heavy-lidded grayness. At the same time, I was struggling to get rid of a build-up of parasites accumulated from years of two-thirds-world travel and living among the poor.

These problems notwithstanding, Deanna and I excitedly prepared to deploy to Phnom Penh in April 1994. We planned to pioneer a team there that would include Dave and Lisa Everitt, Phil Vetter and Sue Lloyd. And yet, I could only say I was excited in the most detached sense. For me, the anticipation of moving to Cambodia to fulfill years of hopes tasted flatly of ash and carried the whiff of the graveyard, when just the opposite should have been the case. I did not yet have the language to articulate it, much less diagnose it, but I was laboring under and struggling against a profound depression.

By September 1993, I knew I was in trouble but didn't know where to turn.

A Minefield of Expectations

Then a marvelous change of events occurred in October 1993, when we discovered that Deanna was pregnant. For a few days we were jubilant, and my emotional skies cleared. Then Deanna began to spot. We called doctors and held on in hope. Waiting.

About the third day, Deanna and I were prayerfully waiting to see if her pregnancy would survive. I was reading in Luke 8 about the disciples out on the water, overcome by a violent storm, with Jesus asleep. I suspected that God was communicating with us. I took heart, reading how Jesus awoke, stilled the storm, chided the disciples for their lack of faith, and they proceeded to cross over. I seized on the image of the boat crossing over as a signal that Deanna's "stormy" pregnancy would likewise cross to the other side and touch shore. I was cautiously elated but also sensed God's telling me not to share this with Deanna. Nevertheless, I told Deanna the substance of my quiet time with the Lord.

Deanna miscarried a day and a half later. For nearly two weeks afterward, I spoke with God only listlessly. I felt deeply betrayed. Why had God allowed me to form such a damaging expectation that our baby would survive? Finally, I let Him catch up to me. I sensed Him whispering to me, "You're angry with Me. I know this. But you misunderstood My message through the story of the disciples in the boat. My message wasn't that you would cross over. My message was that in the storm, I was with you in the boat."

"I was in the boat," I breathed aloud, feeling the phrase's impact. I started to cry, alone in the room, weeping cleanly for the first time in several weeks.

The miscarriage served as the straw that broke the camel's back. By January 1994, I was emotionally flatlined and struggling just to get up in the morning. Once I could articulate all the symptoms I was experiencing in one overall description, my doctors were able to diagnose my condition: depression. I immediately sought help in counseling and came away with greater understanding of depression as an affliction. I also learned how to develop better coping skills and how to reduce the impact my depression exerted on others. Deanna and I were forced to admit that I would not be an asset as pioneering team leader alongside her in Phnom Penh. That was a painful recognition. Instead, the Everitts pioneered the Cambodia team in June 1994. Deanna and I moved out of our Cambodian complex in Long Beach and into a focused role for a year in which we concentrated on developing InnerCHANGE as an order, forming our leaders, and attending to healing.

The Fingerprint of Pain

I don't know what it's like to bury a spouse, all your children, even much of your extended family, as our Cambodian mother, Ohm, did.

And, learning from my own battle with depression, which brings with it kinds of pain that often defy description, I have learned to be cautious about saying the five words that sometimes come quite naturally: "I know how you feel." I believe that each fingerprint of pain is unique.

In his masterful work *The Solace of Fierce Landscapes,* Belden Lane describes the personal boundary he could not completely cross in gently caring for his dying mother: "The concluding period of her life taught me that the most intimate (and enigmatic) moments of any of our lives are essentially closed to what we call 'experience.' They can no more be grasped and defined than the desert itself."[44]

I don't know that those insights forged in pain are more valuable than are others. I do know that they *feel* like they are, and that is a treasure of consolation.

In my struggle, not only with depression but also chronic physical pain and the pain of loss, I often turned to the story of Job. In joining Job in confronting his counselors' fortune-cookie platitudes, I began to see that my pain wasn't necessarily a personal rebuke from God. I began to forge a more authentic, less self-conscious faith than I'd known before. Job's fervent declaration, "Though he slay me, yet I will hope in him" (Job 13:15), was a confirmation for me of my own bedrock. I did not fully understand my depression or some of the losses I had suffered, and I was not resigned to them. But in the turbulence, I realized that the eye of the storm was God, and my immovable hope was alive in Him.

I also found encouragement in the apostle James's counsel in the first sentence of his book, that when positively embraced, trials test one's faith in a way that yields perseverance. Though at times I feared that I was getting more bitter than better, I was able to discern that dealing with depression was lending depth to my faith.

This insight harmonized with another truth, from David in Psalm 51, that a broken heart was an acceptable sacrifice to bring to God as often as it was authentically experienced. Until my severe depression in the early '90s, I had understood a broken heart to be something to take to God for consolation. I had never before seen it ennobled as a sacrifice of praise.

Finally, depression put me in personal touch with the substance of Philippians 3:10, in which Paul describes a "fellowship" we have with Christ in *His* sufferings. This was immensely valuable to me because it helped me develop a healthy detachment from pain. Pain can be excessively personal and inward-directing. This verse liberated me from the possessiveness of pain while at the same time it released me into the dignity of Christ's fellowship.

A Sea of Red

Nate and Jenny Bacon were gathered with about 60 young people at the edge of an ex-gang member's grave in San Francisco. They also stood collectively and symbolically at the edge of releasing their friend Angel, a 19-year-old young man cut down in a gang shooting that should never have included him.

Nate played a lead role in the service. His memories of that day are powerful but disjointed—vivid frames loosely accompanied by a wailing in his soul. He told me he could remember looking out at a sea of red, as Angel's former gang and others connected to the gang gathered, dressed in tribute. He remembers speaking at the service and looking across at the faces of InnerCHANGE staff. Angel's funeral was a gathering of clans, or more accurately, families. InnerCHANGE, San Dimas, St. Peter's, the gang, and at the center of it all, Angel's mother, Esperanza, burying her only son.

Spoken prayers finished, unspoken ones taking shape, Angel's body was lowered into the ground. First came handfuls of dirt, then showers of red roses and bandanas. As the last of the earth was gathered to the grave, some of Angel's friends from the street drifted away down the rows of stones, off-balance with shock and grief, looking for other friends who had been killed on the streets.

Two of the graves they sought were those of the young men whose violent deaths in 1992 had compelled our San Francisco community to found San Dimas, a ministry to gang members and inmates at San Francisco's Juvenile Hall (YGC).

The day our San Dimas team buried Angel, they buried more than a young man. As Nate shared with me years later, "Once in a while in ministry you get a chance to see the answer to what feels like all your best hopes and dreams. Angel was that answer for me."

When he committed himself to the Lord, Angel courageously and completely turned his life around. He immediately became an inspiring model for his gang friends and a highly relevant model of a bridge to possibilities beyond gang life. Nate and Jenny first connected with Angel at YGC a year before he was released. They came to love him as a son and also became very close to his mother and sister. Just a few months before he was shot, Angel traveled with the Bacon family to a mission conference in Europe, because that was how he saw himself, as a missionary. Perhaps the most moving occasion for them during those travels was visiting the underground chamber that Church tradition considers to be the death-row cell for the apostles Peter and Paul. The Bacons were struck by the message on a plaque posted there, declaring the blood of the martyrs to be the seed of the Church. Looking back, Nate wonders if God was preparing them for Angel's death, even then.

So many hopes and dreams for Angel's future impact for the Kingdom were buried in a sea of red roses and bandanas that September day. Before that, there was the red stain on the pavement, and the blood that swept out the door in the hospital room in impossible quantities as physicians performed aggressive last-ditch procedures to revive Angel. Nate had snuck back into the emergency room in which Angel lay. If he had had any doubts that Angel was lost to them, the sight of his body torn open dispelled them.

The night Angel was shot, Cryfirst called with the news. Nate had just gotten home from the dinner that marked the passage of first-year InnerCHANGE apprentices graduating and new ones coming in. Augustín, a former gang-banger trying to go straight and living with the Bacons as a foster son, answered the phone. Augustín choked out the news of Angel's shooting. Jenny reacted as much to the look in Augustín's face as to the news itself and cried out, "Not Angel!"

Nate went next door to José Peñate's apartment, who received the news with a grave calm. José had had several dreams that week indicating that Angel might be shot but would survive. Nate and José ran to the corner of Potrero and 25th. Homeboys and homegirls clustered there, weeping, at the site already sealed off with yellow tape. A patrol car pulled up, and an officer called out hopefully, "Looks like they might be able to save your friend."

Nate glanced at José and said, "Go get Esperanza." After that, Nate went to the hospital. When he arrived, a doctor confided gently that they had done all they could to save Angel, but a bullet to the left aorta had killed him instantly. Nate began to sob uncontrollably. The doctor asked him who he was.

"I'm his pastor," he managed.

"You're his pastor?" he questioned in mild surprise. Perhaps he was concerned that Nate's out-of-control grief would not go far to comfort anyone else, especially Angel's mother, who was on the way to the hospital.

Nate went out into the waiting room, knowing that he would have to deliver the news to Esperanza, the news every mother whose child is connected to gangs dreads to hear. In the hall, a young gang member waited, trembling.

"This has to stop," Nate declared firmly.

"I can't change," the teenager responded gravely, shaking his head hopelessly. The reality of gang addiction came home to Nate with new conviction.

Nate is one who has always been noted as being slow to anger. But in the days immediately following the funeral, the pain he experienced drove him to a rage he could not control. When he found himself passing Sureño gang members on the streets, he would lean out the window of his battered van and "mad-dog" them, that is, stare ominously. The Sureños were the gang responsible for killing Angel. Nate was overtaken with righteous fury at the injustice that Angel, who had gone straight and was doing so much good, should be mistaken and cut down as a Norteño.

Years later, Nate confessed that immediately following Angel's killing, he experienced something of what it is to become a gang member. Seeking vengeance is obligatory for gang members. Indeed, it is automatic. He found himself assuming the dehumanizing mind-set that made him feel that the Sureños, that any or *all* of them, needed to pay, not just the four young men charged with shooting Angel.

Nate's wake-up call came while he was sitting in St. Peter's chapel in the midst of other mourners during Angel's novena. (In Catholic tradition, family and friends gather together to pray during the nine days following a burial. This is called a novena.)

He sensed from God that he could not release his dehumanizing anger, fueled by this vivid sense of corporate injury on behalf of Esperanza, members of San Dimas and Angel's friends and "homies," apart from meeting one of Angel's killers face to face. Nate wasn't exactly sure what he should do, but he knew it required human contact.

He drove to 850 Bryant, the holding facility in which the oldest killer was locked up. This young man was the only one of the four young men who was over 18. Nate sat outside in his van for a half hour, not so much in indecision as in gathering a willingness to proceed. Once inside the doors, he waited another half hour. Finally, Nate signed in as a pastor. Going up in the elevator, it hit him, "Will I recognize this young man from the street?"

He didn't. The police brought out a young man who warily looked around; they uncuffed him and then locked him and Nate inside a conference room. Waiting an hour had not clarified for Nate what he needed to say. He stumbled over an introduction, describing the ministry of San Dimas. The young man regarded Nate blankly. Finally, Nate dove in and shared that Angel had been like a son and was a member of the San Dimas ministry.

The young man put up his hands as if expecting a verbal assault, and declaimed, "I cannot talk about my case."

"That's okay, I know," Nate replied. "I just want to tell you a little bit about Angel."

As Nate proceeded to tell Angel's story, the young man began to tear up. In the course of their interaction, both were able to regain a sense of humanity. This young man now knew something of Angel as an individual, not simply as a gang target. And now Nate could put a human face on Angel's killers, and in so doing, he could no longer maintain his violent sense of right-eous outrage toward the Sureños. "When I get out, I want to visit Angel's grave," the young man said quietly. They stood up, shook hands and hugged with authentic emotion.

Nate never saw this young man again. He thought he might go back to visit him at some point, but perhaps he had already gone as far as his grief would allow. Recently, Nate learned that this man has become a Christian and is doing as well as can be hoped for in a maximum-security facility.

With Angel's death, a dozen or more of Angel's friends final-ly closed the door on gang life, including the young man who prophesied in the hospital room that he'd never change. The pain of Angel's loss is still there for all of us in InnerCHANGE, independent of the amazing redemptive work his death ushered in. Angel was, and continues to be, a missionary powerfully used by God.

A Message to Communities

It is not always automatic for people experiencing loss or pain to draw strength from community. This is, perhaps, especially true of men, who tend to withdraw and lick their wounds in private. There are others whose first instincts might be to lean into community but, on second thought, determine that the risk of being misunderstood or of being overwhelmed with sen-timent is too great.

In general, communities manifest their care to people in pain most effectively through presence rather than words. Even the right words can be difficult to process for some people who are in pain.

Protected

Laila Blanchard

It's one of the most disturbing nightmares from my time in Venezuela. I am asleep in my small blue room with a tin roof. A square piece of the wall is being cut out. In no time, a gun is pointing at me through the hole.

I awake in a panic, imagining a *malandro* (gangster) entering my room with malice. What would I do if it were really happening? Would I struggle to get the gun from him? Rebuke him in the name of Jesus? Cower in the corner? Or maybe some combination of the three?

Several months pass. I am thirsty. It has been a hot, long day. I've got a little bit of a cold virus, so I want some orange juice. It is 10 minutes before 8:00 P.M., and I head toward the neighborhood corner store. As I am standing in line to call out *"jugo de naranja"* to the store attendant, I hear gunfire within 10 feet. I see a pregnant woman throw herself down behind a 1970s lime-green car, and I instinctively do the same. The ringing from the shots stops, a group of young men runs off, and there is some yelling. The pregnant woman and I slowly pick ourselves up, dusting off our clothes.

I can feel my face go white. And my throat is even drier than before. I am not worried, just dazed. Surveying the scene around me, still in line for my orange juice, I see Ricardo. I live in Ricardo's home. He lives with his mother-in-law and his common-law wife and his five children, and lots more people. We are a full house.

He grabs my arm and pulls me away from where I am standing in shock. He understands that whatever I was in line to buy is not as important as leaving this scene of danger. His steps are even and quick, and he looks back occasionally.

We walk down the winding street to a large group gathered outside, where a neighborhood church is having an outdoor service. Ricardo safely deposits me inside the group like a mother hen with her chick.

Somehow I feel comforted through Ricardo's firm grasp taking me by the arm and moving me down the street and into the middle of a throng. It is really hard to know how we will react in the face of real danger. It turns out that I just followed after a pregnant woman and a young father. I was brought into the strength of others. *

Gifted communities also keep a sharp eye out for opportunities to genuinely celebrate even mundane things in a way that helps pain stay in perspective without being diminished. It is amazing how often passages in Scripture combine notions of rejoicing and pain in the same sentence. Celebration is not merely an instinctive response; it can be an offensive weapon for communities shadowed with disappointment. Much can be written on this subject, but my central purpose here is to affirm that gifted, caring communities can truly help people in pain struggle forward in ways that keep them in touching distance of the Lord. The community members benefit, too, in expressing genuine care, as their faith is built up in the living incarnation of the ministering Body of Christ.

Generally, it is best for communities to establish an environment of open dialogue in addition to quality care, in which all members can be understood and mentored in what it means to care for a person in pain. Occasionally, mission communities can become so enmeshed in division or are beyond their depth in skill that the most redemptive way to proceed is to bring in a non-team member with skills in conflict resolution. In any case, caring for people in pain will be an abiding concern and at times a source of tension for apostolic communities among the poor, even though their primary missional focus is the neighborhood residents, not themselves. Communities, or teams, tend to go through organizational phases and exhibit fairly common corporate behaviors regardless of size. It behooves team leaders to have some skill and experience in team dynamics and conflict resolution.

The most effective thing a mission community can do to guard against unhealthy division is to head off unhealthy sources of pain from the outset. I believe that the source of much unhealthy pain derives from team members setting unrealistic expectations of themselves and each other. The starting place is *not* to proceed from the premise that expectations are hazardous or wrong and try to hold one another loosely without expectations. This is both unhealthy and impossible. High expectations that are also realistic energize a team. The Bible illustrates this concept many times in the experience of Jesus with His high-expectation community of disciples. The point is, expectations of teammates do harm when they are *unrealistic*, not when they are big or small.

Some of the natural but most troubling expectations that community members form of one another relate to our very identities. In Scripture we see that people formed wrong expectations despite the active presence of the Spirit of God. Luke 3:15 gives us a good example by observing that in a "state of expectation"(*NASB*) some wondered if John the Baptist might be the Christ.

We have found that the best way to set realistic expectations of each other up front is to work hard at knowing one another. Many unrealistic expectations are set, despite the presence of real appreciation engineered by the Spirit, because we mistake each other to possess qualities we don't have. And then we cause each other pain when we don't measure up to those imagined expectations. I find it helpful to recall Jesus' model as He created a climate of open dialogue and discovery among His disciples when He launched a discussion on expectations of His identity with, "Who do people say that I am?" (see Matt. 16). He continued to press, asking, "But who do you say that I am?" In this team discussion, I believe the Lord was trying to surface expectations and align them with reality such that His choice to walk toward the cross would be understood.

Phnom Penh Redux, 1995

Early in 1995, I traveled to Phnom Penh to check in on our team. Emotionally, I had gained enough altitude from depression to return, and the visit was timely for the team as well. I cleared customs and found myself a bit anxious, wondering how it would feel to be back in a country that had at one time been a heartfelt personal destination. I stepped out into a wall of moist, pungent air and immediately saw Dave atop his motorcycle, arms folded, smiling broadly. His head was wrapped in a Cambodian *krama*. It doesn't get better than riding with Dave, a former professional dirt-bike rider, through a country as fascinating as Cambodia, even if it's just a trip from the airport.

I asked about Pastor Kakedaa. Dave told me that Kakedaa was training young church planters in central Phnom Penh. I couldn't resist going there to surprise my friend. Neither could I resist the opportunity to see him training new pastoral leaders from all over the country. So Dave turned his bike in the direction of Phnom Penh. We slipped into the back of the upper room Kakedaa was teaching in, and he nearly fell over mid-sentence. He announced a break as soon as he could. We went outside where he bear-hugged me so hard that I was sure my ribs had cracked.

I broached the subject of the woman we'd prayed for two years before. I wasn't sure what I wanted—details, closure. For a moment, Kakedaa tried to remember the woman—he and I had done so much together two years before. I nudged his memory along, describing the night before the airport, the tall building, the woman's head swaying rhythmically side to side.

"Oh, that woman," he said, smiling in recognition. "Yes, she's better. She is still confined to her bed, but she's added weight. Not long after we were there, some of her family became Christians. They go to the church in Psaa Tmai."

I stood for a moment, bracing myself as though wading into a rising tide.

The woman who had died was another woman, an *old* woman we'd met only once, Kakedaa clarified. Dave, Pastor Kakedaa and I again rode over to the tall building in central Phnom Penh and prayed for the woman and her family. She greeted me almost as if expecting me and asked about Deanna. She had indeed gained weight. Equally important, she had regained her identity as a woman—a woman confined, certainly, but no longer a woman defined by her condition.

She had not physically walked away from her bed, but in a very real sense, she had indeed risen.

the subconscious church

For from now on, the goods which have been bestowed upon the
ornaments of the idols such as these, will be turned, if God wills,
to the poor, who are the true images of God.

HULDRYCH ZWINGLI (1525)

Poor communities are often seen as social cul-de-sacs—places we
try to avoid. As missionaries among the needy, however, we have
discovered that these landscapes are peopled with individuals
whose stories need telling. Each person has his or her own fascinating biography. The fact that biographies of the poor rarely
make it into our mainstream media is a tragic loss. Poverty often
grabs coverage in its horrific aggregate face while the individual
lives of poor people remain invisible to us, and their histories go
into unmarked graves.

Unfortunately it seems to have always been this way. The
poor do not factor into the writing of history, despite the fact

that they are making it. As medieval scholar Michel Mollat notes, the poor rarely show up in recorded history except in social eruptions. I am reminded of the 1992 Los Angeles riots, a time when the faces of people living in the ghettoes of South Central and Long Beach flickered briefly across our TV screens. Still, as Mollat points out, even when poor people become subjects of historical writing, "the writer rarely adopts the poor man's point of view."[45]

And yet, I have long suspected that from the bottom-up point of view, the poor and those who work among them occupy an essential place in Kingdom history. I find that most Christians, rich and poor alike, intuit that if history is recorded in eternity, it will look upside-down compared to the history the world records. Eternal history will not be impressed with power, or preoccupied with celebrity, but will, instead, celebrate the lowly. This history will describe a Kingdom reflecting the psalms: The needy will be vindicated and the hurting compassionately delivered.

There is a Kingdom that we are to seek devotedly. It is so fair, so full, that its single-minded pursuit will bring into alignment all other needs, all other grails (see Matt. 6:33-34). We know this from God's Word, but we sense it instinctively as well when we consider people like Mother Teresa. When I listen to people speak about her, including those who are not following Christ, I find that she inspires more than admiration and stirs more than guilt. The radiance of Mother Teresa's life reminds us that there is a place better than the one we are in, the dimensions of which we cannot see but can dimly discern as a place prepared that will feel like home.

Mother Teresa's selfless example is a reference point that shows us that a Micah 6:8 life of mercy, justice and intimacy with Jesus is possible. She is also a reminder that numbers of faithful men and women came before her, in the nearly 2,000 years that separate the New Testament biblical record from our current age. Subconsciously, I know that these men and women are out there, illustrating the presence of the kingdom of God, even though I cannot give many of them names and faces. I have come to call this body of missional experience the "sub-conscious church," because even though I cannot summon it in detail, I know that it exists, I know what it stands for, and I know that it influences me. Brushing up against the sub-conscious church communicates more than historical scenery; it gives me hope and shapes my values.

Messages From the Sub-conscious Church

As a research fellow at Yale in 1998 and 1999, during a year's sabbatical, I decided to delve into the anonymous archives of the sub-conscious church. I wanted to mine history for direction as we moved forward as communities among the poor—to "let the dead vote," as G. K Chesterton put it. Yale Divinity School has an amazing library, and I spent hours there in passionate pursuit of an upside-down melody expressed over and over in individual lives. The research became deeply personal, as if I were witnessing the unfolding of a spiritual genealogy. I was looking for my generation's spiritual ancestors who had followed Christ to the margins and witnessed Him proclaim again:

The Spirit of the Lord is on me, because he has anointed me to preach good news to the poor. He has sent me to proclaim freedom for the prisoners and recovery of sight to the blind, to release the oppressed, to proclaim the year of the Lord's favor (Luke 4:18-19).

The Bishops

I was not disappointed in my search. Early in the history of the Church, leaders considered the work of caring for the poor so essential to following Christ that they coined a phrase that was to guide the Church almost to the modern era. It helped prefigure and underwrite reform during the Protestant and Catholic Reformations beginning in the sixteenth century. It states that "the property of the church is the patrimony of the poor." In A.D. 511, the bishops present at the First Council of Orléans agreed that urban churches should set aside one-quarter of their income for the needs of the poor. In rural parishes, the standard was raised to one-third. At that time, it was assumed that the bishop would take in the needy such that the bishop's chambers and the "poorhouse" were one and the same. (Michel Mollat and other scholars would say that this was tacitly understood by all bishops, though perhaps unevenly practiced.) These assumptions about the nature of the Church's responsibility to the poor were considered such givens that when they were violated, public uproar ensued. St. Ambrose, in particular, railed against church leaders who held back more than the church's percentage of offerings for the poor, calling them "murderers of the poor."[46] I find it interesting that this progressive thinking about the poor was emerging at a time when the Roman world order was giving way to the Dark Ages in the Western world.

The Celts

The Celtic missionaries originating from Ireland present a profoundly inspiring model for mission entities among the poor, particularly for orders. In the sixth and seventh centuries, as the Roman world order continued to disintegrate, Irish missionaries evangelized much of Britain and made important inroads into Western Europe. In contrast to increasingly inward-focused Roman church leaders, bands of Celtic missionaries were motivated by a primitive but profound apostolic mission to evangelize. They lived communally and maintained extremely simple lifestyles so as not to distract from the simplicity of the Jesus message they proclaimed.[47]

Of these Celts, St. Cuthbert (died 687), in particular, fascinates me. Born into a well-known family and mentored by Aidan at Lindisfarne in Anglo-Saxon Northumbria, Cuthbert traveled into the remotest reaches of Northeastern Britain and into the most indigent "hamlets . . . other men had dreaded to visit [because] of their poverty and up-landish rudeness."[48] He was a mystic whose work among the poor proceeded from his intimacy with Christ. Often, he could be found singing the psalms with gusto in freezing seawater up to his knees. Cuthbert was so beloved by the powerful and the powerless alike that he was reverenced for generations after his death. More than a century later, the Lindisfarne monks wandered seven years with his body to protect it from Viking raiders.[49]

The Reformers

I learned that there were numerous heroic efforts to reform the medieval Church before the Reformations of the sixteenth century. Time and again, the Church's accumulated wealth and neglect of the poor were issues central to the reformers. These attempts at reform were only partially successful, because power and patronage in the medieval Church were deeply entrenched. Bernard of Clairvaux (1090-1153) prophetically called the Church back to its mission among the poor while simultaneously warning against the misuse of wealth in excessively ornamenting the church. The church, he observed, "clothes her stones in gold and leaves her sons naked."[50]

In the sixteenth century, against the backdrop of one of the most dynamic periods in religious history, the Protestant and Catholic Reformations were undergirded by fresh pursuit of the Kingdom and, consequently, concern for the poor. It was a time when the faithfulness of whole communities, even entire cities, was resurging. Huldrych Zwingli's Zurich offers an especially compelling example.

Zwingli championed the notion of the poor as the image of God and challenged the city to respond corporately. Zurich embarked on one of the most vigorous and ambitious welfare programs in history, selling church art and lavish ornamentation to feed the poor who represented Christ. In January 1525, Zurich's church leaders arrayed poor people in traditional priestly robes and instructed them to carry on with their daily lives in the city. This both illustrated and confirmed critical changes Zurich had made: that the poor were the image of Christ and that the image of Christ belonged in the world, not simply in the church.[51]

The Friars

Wherever I looked in my historical research, I came away encouraged that throughout the ages, God actively raised up followers in the simple but profound path of loving mercy, doing justice and abiding with one's God. The period in history that I studied most was the thirteenth and fourteenth centuries and the emergence of the friars. Like a well-worn book that falls open to a certain page, time and again I came back to how God used these dedicated men and women. In choosing lives of complete poverty, they breathed new dignity into the lives of the poor. Furthermore, in a time when the Church's presentation of the gospel had become increasingly remote, the friars recaptured the essence of the good news, living Jesus-style lives of concrete discipleship in ways that poor people and laypersons everywhere could see, hear and touch. They experienced a vital sustaining intimacy with Jesus among the poor that transformed society, high and low, from the thirteenth century through the fifteenth century.

Even with a separation of nearly 800 years, I found that the colossal presence of St. Francis, and his uncomplicated devotion to Jesus, still shook the world. St. Francis and his early followers challenged traditional notions of helping the poor, moving the Church *beyond charity* to take on the lifestyle of the poor and intentionally keep company with them. Adopting a simple lifestyle among the poor was more than a strategy to reach the marginalized. It flowed from an understanding that Christ's face could be glimpsed in the faces of the poor, and that their dependency illustrated Christ's utter dependence on His Father.[52]

There is a story about a young Dominican friar that has been passed down for centuries that evokes a sense of this sub-conscious church. It is often attributed to Thomas Aquinas. Thomas Aquinas left the Church a monumental legacy of thought that included his best-known synthesis of doctrine, Summa Theologiae.

The version of the story I recall is that a young Thomas Aquinas, newly established in the Dominican order, journeyed from Paris to Rome to gain an audience with the pope. He arrived in the opulent outer court of the papal palace and was sternly told to wait by a sumptuously dressed cleric bent over a schedule. Thomas waited. Several hours passed. Finally the cleric came back to admit Thomas. The cleric took in the bare feet and the well-traveled black robe, as if seeing Thomas for the first time. In an unguarded moment, the official's eye traveled from Thomas to the gilded, vaulted ceiling and opulent ornamentation of the papal court, and back to Thomas again.

"I suppose the Church can no longer say, 'Silver and gold have we none,'" the official muttered with an attempt at pride.

"Perhaps that is the reason the Church also cannot say, 'Take up your bed, rise, and walk,'" Thomas shot back.

This story, popularly bequeathed from generation to generation, may be one of the more memorable stories associated with him, or it may be apocryphal. But in a story of this nature, fact is not the point. The truth is in the meaning of the story, and the meaning is clear: The affluence of the medieval Church cost it dearly in spiritual influence. For me, this is a tale from the subconscious church passed down through the centuries as a living reminder that we, the people of God, must not serve two masters; we must seek the Kingdom first. ✳

It was oddly comforting, also, to be reminded that these men and women weren't all impossibly larger-than-life figures with industrial-strength faith. The friars were not always completely Kingdom-dominated in their interaction as mission entities. As I followed their journey, I found that there were times when the Dominicans and Franciscans, specifically, rivaled one another for influence in certain cities, and at other times competed to assert who had the best claim to the pure evangelical life deriving from lifestyles of complete poverty.[53]

Within decades of their founding, the Franciscans, Dominicans and Poor Clares numbered in the thousands, and within 50 years they were proclaiming the good news to the most remote corners of the globe. Could this missional phenomenon happen again? Could apostolic living among the poor spark renewal in the same way God used the lives of the friars in the thirteenth and fourteenth centuries? I asked myself this question in study on sabbatical and continue to ask it prayerfully today. As I travel in the two-thirds world and become increasingly connected through the Bakke Graduate University to men and women ministering in the margins, performing the work of holistically raising disciples, planting churches, and transforming communities, I am greatly encouraged.

As I look at the West, particularly the United States, I am also optimistic, but more cautiously so. I believe that we could see an outpouring of men and women who would devote seasons of their lives and more to ministry among the poor. But I also believe that our cultural materialism exerts such gravitational pull that many may try short-term stints among the poor, though few will be able to break free from this pervasive materialistic way of life to commit long-term.

Downward Rising

Jim Bloom

Not all that is valued as gold
Glitters and dazzles the eyes
Not all that would lead to life
Is seen by the great to be wise
Not all that is lauded as strength
Is gained by the sword that we swing
And those who inherit the earth
Will ascend by a downward rising

Cloaked in the folly of lowliness
Veiled wisdom makes its way
Below the gaze of the great ones
On the road to a downward rising
The powers cannot perceive
The one without a desire
To possess and to dominate
But who'll die in a downward rising

With the malice of pride unleashed
Seeming weakness to exploit
The demons of fear and hate
Are exposed to a downward rising

Yet the deeds that will prove to move
The wheels that change the world
Are designed to be performed
In the way of a downward rising

We continue to approach the poor with a split personality in the West, alternating between compassion and indifference. I question whether our understanding of discipleship and our concept of leadership aren't radically different from the discipleship and leadership expressed in St. Francis's day and militate against a collective obedience to God on a scale witnessed in the Middle Ages. Perhaps these questions are better asked against the backdrop of two biblical stories.

One Faith, Two Crowds

I turn now to two passages that illustrate our natural ambivalence to the poor and that point to the ongoing need to found and sustain mission communities that intentionally minister among the poor. Both passages are from Luke, both are about men of unusual faith in need, and both are about Jesus' compassionate response in healing.

> When Jesus had finished saying all this in the hearing of the people, he entered Capernaum. There, a centurion's servant, whom his master valued highly, was sick and about to die. The centurion heard of Jesus and sent some elders of the Jews to him, asking him to come and heal his servant. When they came to Jesus, they pleaded earnestly with him, "This man deserves to have you do this, because he loves our nation and has built our synagogue." So Jesus went with them.
>
> He was not far from the house when the centurion sent friends to say to him: "Lord, don't trouble yourself,

for I do not deserve to have you come under my roof. That is why I did not even consider myself worthy to come to you. But say the word and my servant will be healed. For I myself am a man under authority, with soldiers under me. I tell this one, 'Go,' and he goes; and that one, 'Come,' and he comes. I say to my servant, 'Do this,' and he does it.

When Jesus heard this, he was amazed at him, and turning to the crowd following him, he said, "I tell you, I have not found such great faith even in Israel." Then the men who had been sent returned to the house and found the servant well (Luke 7:1-10).

This story takes place in the year 28 and is about a man from Capernaum. This man was no ordinary man. He was a Roman soldier, a conqueror in a subordinated land. And he was no ordinary Roman soldier but a centurion.

By definition, a centurion commanded 100 soldiers. But by this late date in the Roman Empire's journey, centurions were more often commanding thousands of men. They had become the stuff of legend, because they were responsible for the hands-on command of the toughest and most successful troops the world had ever seen.

However, Luke's account shows us that this centurion was exceptional in both his cross-cultural sensitivity and in his humility toward Jesus. He understood authority as a two-way street—something to be under as well as to exercise.

A word about Palestine: Viewed from the perspective of the Roman Empire's high command, Palestine was a tiny pesthole in a comparatively smooth imperial road. Roman authorities considered the Jews a violent people serving a backward, tribal God. Thus, Palestine was a hardship post. It was where Rome sent young men with no connections and old men who had failed or been disgraced.

Occasionally, very occasionally, Rome dispatched a genuinely gifted commander to Palestine, simply to keep order. Luke gives the impression that this centurion was one of these. Though Palestine was a difficult place to be posted, and hardly an asset to a rising career, this centurion evidently did not become bitter. Instead, he seems to have fallen in love with the Jewish people and their God, even going so far as to build a synagogue.

The centurion had power, money and prestige, but he also had compassion, humility and cultural sensitivity. He had all the credentials of a person everyone wanted to get to know, despite the fact that he was Roman.

And it seemed that everyone did know him. On this particular day, when the centurion's slave was very sick, the centurion had no difficulty finding advocates who would petition Jesus on his behalf. The centurion not only had Jewish friends to send, but he also had the *right* Jewish friends to send in order to communicate appropriately with a man of authentic authority. He was able to prevail upon the elders in Capernaum. Naturally, the elders were eager to go to Jesus on the centurion's behalf and assure Him that this particular Roman was worthy.

The centurion had never met Jesus, but he knew and admired Him from reputation. As a man of substantive authority himself, he recognized in Jesus a man of even greater authority. Consequently, when he learned that Jesus was on the way to his home, he began to have serious misgivings about taking up

Jesus' valuable time. So he gathered up yet another group of Jewish friends to intercept Jesus on the road and ask Him to heal his servant from a distance. Perhaps, too, in dispatching this second group, the centurion was hastened by the urgency of his beloved servant's condition.

In any case, Jesus was greatly impressed by the centurion's intensity of faith and understanding of authority, especially as a non-Jew. He exclaimed, "Not even in Israel have I found such great faith."

Jesus healed the servant. No doubt the centurion was pleased. The elders were pleased. All the friends gathered into this extra-ordinary drama have to have gone away satisfied, not simply because a dying man was healed, but because they played an affirming and assisting role in the event. This was compassion scripted at its socially acceptable best.

I should note, however, that it is the centurion who is proclaimed worthy—not the slave. The Jewish leaders ask Jesus to heal the slave inasmuch as they want to be able to help the master. I am not sure that the slave, as a man in need, entered the calculations of anyone except for Jesus and the centurion. And inasmuch as the Roman leader was a generous philanthropist, is it conceivable that the Jewish leaders found motive for asking Jesus to heal the slave in a bit of a "real world" payback? This is, perhaps, a stretch, but the issue of the slave's intrinsic (and unstated) worthiness helps to introduce the second story.

Not an Officer, Not a Gentleman
This second story also recounts a meeting between Jesus and a man of faith in need. It takes place near Jericho, two years after Jesus healed the centurion's servant.

As Jesus approached Jericho, a blind man was sitting by the roadside begging. When he heard the crowd going by, he asked what was happening. They told him, "Jesus of Nazareth is passing by."

He called out, "Jesus, son of David, have mercy on me!"

Those who led the way rebuked him and told him to be quiet, but he shouted all the more, "Son of David, have mercy on me!"

Jesus stopped and ordered the man to be brought to him. When he came near, Jesus asked him, "What do you want me to do for you?"

"Lord, I want to see," he replied.

Jesus said to him, "Receive your sight; your faith has healed you." Immediately he received his sight and followed Jesus, praising God. When all the people saw it, they also praised God (Luke 18:35-42).

To understand the full impact of this story, it is helpful to remember that by the year 30, the Lord was rapidly approaching the close of His mission. Luke is explicit in telling us that this was Jesus' last trip to Jerusalem—the goal was in sight. The Bible tells us that Jesus resolutely set His face toward the city and the cross (see Luke 9:51; 18:31-33). If ever there was a time when Jesus deserved to be single-minded and not stop for any distractions, surely, this was the day.

As in the story of the centurion, Jesus was traveling in the company of His disciples and an entourage of well-wishers. I imagine that as He approached Jericho, a crowd gathered. Jesus was sighted; excitement traveled like a lit fuse. On this day, in this crowd, Jesus would specially touch one man.

Who was he? Unlike the centurion, this man was not a local hero. However, he was a man of faith. Few recognized his faith, because he had not acquired it in the conventional arenas of power and authority. He had gained faith from depending day by day upon God for his very survival. This man was blind. And because he was blind, he could not work, and so, had to beg. Every day this beggar, named Bartimaeus, lived by grace through faith that God would cause men to notice him.

We are told little about Bartimaeus. We do not know his age, where he was born or if he was born blind. We may suspect that he was not born blind, because he told Jesus he wanted to *regain* his sight. Still, the information we have on Bartimaeus is minimal compared with what we know about the centurion. I wonder if the Spirit inspired Luke to leave the details out so that Bartimaeus would forever remain an archetype for every generation that would pass him by. Bartimaeus is every home-less man, every beggar, reaching out a sunburned, smudged hand the world over.

But we do know this man's name—Bartimaeus. Unlike the centurion, the Spirit inspired Luke to give us this beggar's name. He is archetypal, but real. He was a poor man, not simply an abstract representation of poverty. We know the centurion by his merits; we know Bartimaeus by his name. In this, I think we can glimpse the upside-down Kingdom at work.

Bartimaeus cried out for Jesus. The crowd restrained him. He cried out louder.

Despite the fact that Jesus' heart and mind were set on the cross, He stopped. He saw Bartimaeus's need and asked him what He would have Him do. He saw that Bartimaeus possessed faith, and stretched out His hand. Jesus simply reached out and touched Bartimaeus. No paperwork was involved.

The Instincts of the Crowd

So far, the details of Jesus' encounter here are similar to His encounter with the centurion. Jesus met a man in need, saw that the man had faith and commended that faith. Jesus performed a miracle of healing. Everything is similar, except the crowd's response. The crowd in Bartimaeus's case reacted very differently from the crowd gathered for the centurion. They were ready to pass this beggar by in what my friend Ken Fong calls "a learned blindness."

Unlike the centurion, Bartimaeus had no friends who interceded with Jesus on his behalf. No one came forward to proclaim Bartimaeus worthy. No one even grudgingly helped him get to Jesus. In fact, some actually tried to restrain him. Luke tells us in verse 40 that Jesus had to *command* people to bring this beggar forward. People tumbled over themselves to help the centurion; they tumbled over themselves to hinder Bartimaeus.

There are probably several reasons why the crowd's response to Bartimaeus was out of sync with Jesus' response. I will suggest two.

First, Bartimaeus was not going to make anyone's dinner guest list. Unlike the centurion, he had no money, no power and no prestige. He was not attractive and not pleasant to be around. Most likely, he was also filthy.

It's unfortunate, isn't it? We want to help the poor, but they never seem to look the way we want them to. We want them to appear worthy, deserving, respectful. We want them to be nice. But the poor are not all nice people. Yet to Jesus, Bartimaeus looked okay. He did not mind the stink of a stable; He didn't mind the stink of rags.

The second reason is more subtle and has to do with the way we envision and prioritize "mission." The crowd that accompanied Jesus the day He met Bartimaeus was intent on delivering Him without incident or interruption to Jerusalem. As far as they were concerned, Jerusalem was where everything important was going to take place. On this day, Jerusalem was the mission field. But for Jesus, mission is not exclusively "out there." Mission is always potentially a step away—no farther than a hand's breadth. Bartimaeus was just as important to Jesus as anyone He expected to meet in Jerusalem. He did not delegate this beggar to another; He met Bartimaeus's need Himself.

The disturbing thing about this crowd with Jesus is that they were not bad people. They included Jesus' most trusted disciples and supporters, who wanted to see Jesus come into His kingdom. If interviewed, most would have said they were there to follow Jesus.

Were they? Let's look at Luke 18:39: "Those who led the way rebuked him and told him to be quiet." They were out ahead of Jesus, leading the way.

What can we say in pairing these two stories? I suggest that the centurion rarely struggled to find friends, but Bartimaeus nearly always did. Yet a huge proportion of the world looks more like Bartimaeus than the centurion. We cannot accurately talk about reaching the world without coming to grips with reaching the poor. If we walk by Bartimaeus, we walk by much of the world.

I wonder how often we think we are *following* Jesus, and we assure others that we are following Jesus, when in fact, we are *leading* the way in our lives. Perhaps we're in a hurry to get to Jerusalem or some other place. For us the mission field often seems to be some other place. Whether Jesus is on His way to Jerusalem, Bangkok or Nairobi, I wonder how often we believe we are following Him yet lead Him right by people in need—not because we want to rebel against Jesus, but because we are calling the shots in our lives. We're leading the way, so we put off or postpone people who don't fit our immediate priorities.

I believe that most of the times when we fail Jesus and the needy people He puts in our lives, we don't fail Him on purpose. As I look at my own life, I find that most of the failures, the betrayals even, are not like Judas's deliberate act of disobedience. Many are relatively unconscious, and often they are casual postponements. I wonder what price people in need have paid for my postponements.

I know this: If the people traveling with Jesus on the day He met Bartimaeus had their way, Bartimaeus would have paid with his sight. I'm confident that when we truly position ourselves to follow Jesus, we will stop for the poor when He does. Some of us may even discover that we are called to live our lives among the needy.

Finally, what does this passage about Bartimaeus tell us about leadership and the emphasis we place on it in much of today's world?

The Cult of the Leader

Is our contemporary Western captivation with leaders and leadership development out of balance? Has our emphasis on the cultivation of leadership eclipsed our attention to followership?

The Source of History's Problems

Todd Kennemer

(Written before joining InnerCHANGE as an apprentice)

A conversation I can't forget occurred at the coffee shop when I visited in February. While others were inside playing video games and watching movies, I stayed outside to talk to some people I had met, one of whom called herself "Gadget." Almost every conversation with Gadget revolved around technology, space travel and other dimensions.

Darren asked Gadget that if she were given the chance to travel in time, what time would she choose? She said she would go back 2,000 years and stop Jesus from being born because He is the source of all of history's problems. Skewed as that answer may seem, I came to find out that such hatred and bitterness toward Christ is prevalent among many of the youth the team encounters, and it cemented in my mind the importance of a "presence ministry," one with an agenda not to evangelize and depart, but to care and care some more. Then care again. *

Learning to follow seems to have become a lost art, and yet, Jesus talks far more about following than He does about leading. I don't need to introduce statistics to support the notion that at nearly every level of our culture, from education to sports, we aggressively strive to develop leaders. A casual browse through the main titles of the business/management section of a large bookstore reveals just how many works are dedicated, at least in part, to building effective leaders. I am not sure I have ever seen a book on building followers.

As I reflect on the High Middle Ages in the West, when the Franciscans, Dominicans, Poor Clares and many other mission entities came to the scene, I wonder if people in that period were not more readily disposed to follow Jesus, as opposed to leading on His behalf, than in our own. Certainly it was a less secular time in the Western world, with the concept of Christendom in full flower. In my experience, developing leadership and followership are not mutually exclusive, but complementary, arts. By scripting leadership and followership together, are we not more likely to call forth servant leaders?

What spiritual influence do we miss today by emphasizing leadership at the expense of followership? I wonder what Bartimaeus would tell us?

the challenge

You're here because you know something. What you know you can't explain.
But you feel it. You've felt it your entire life—that there's something wrong in the
world. You don't know what it is, but it's there like a splinter in your mind.
You've been living in a dream world, Neo. This is the world that exists today.
Welcome to the desert of the real.

MORPHEUS TO NEO, *THE MATRIX*

There is a world-class bridge in Kampong Cham, Cambodia, one of the seven cities around the world in which we have placed InnerCHANGE communities. It spans the broad waters of the ancient Mekong River in a perfect silver line. Built shortly after the start of the new millennium by a Japanese firm for $54 million as a gesture of goodwill to the Cambodian people, it is aptly named the Friendship Bridge (above). Because the bridge is the first to cross the Mekong in Cambodia, and because it connects two sections of a central artery, it has quickly become a landmark and point of pride for the Cambodian people.

There is perhaps no clearer portrait of Cambodia's two basic societies, the haves and the have-nots, than this bridge. On top, everyone who is anyone hurries across that bridge, eye on the horizon, straining toward a better economic future. Below the Friendship Bridge, in the netherworld of its pylons, in the sucking muck of the rainy season that hardens to concrete in the dry season, gather the homeless, the dying, the poorest of the poor, straining to eke out a more tolerable present.

God has not called us in InnerCHANGE to minister among the movers and shakers on top of the bridge, as worthy and necessary as that ministry is. He has called us to go below the bridge, into the forsaken shadows and seek out the needy, the neglected, the *moved and shaken*. As much as we can practicably do, God has called us to minister incarnationally.

Beneath the Shoulders of a Great Bridge

Among those moving like shadows beneath the shoulders of the great bridge was a 22-year-old girl named Sopheap. Translated, her name means "Gentle." Her life was anything but. She was homeless, had prostituted herself and been battered to the point that she had become deaf. She was also reportedly dying of AIDS. Diane Moss, founder of Sunrise, InnerCHANGE's home and hospice care for those suffering from AIDS, was alerted to Sopheap's plight in April 2003. She descended with her Khmer staff below the bridge in search of Sopheap, but they were unable to catch up with her.

Diane opened Sunrise to empower impoverished Khmer families to better care for loved ones dying of complications from

AIDS. Within two years, Sunrise included hospice care for the most seriously ill who had been abandoned by families and medical facilities. Sunrise's hospice care wing opened with bed space for six AIDS victims. Sunrise's accomplishment was significant in a country with one of the world's fastest-growing populations afflicted with AIDS. Of equal accomplishment was Diane's determination to minister through the Cambodian churches in Kampong Cham. AIDS sufferers in Cambodia are treated as were lepers in biblical culture. Friends and acquaintances shun them as they would strangers. Their family members, if they do not turn them out on the street, usually keep them well hidden at home, with no outside social contact. Even Cambodian Christians struggle in reaching out to AIDS victims. Beginning with AIDS awareness, Diane patiently worked with the small constellation of churches in Kampong Cham until they were in a position to minister to this terribly isolated population together. Diane's current staff members are all Cambodian nationals, and much of the home visitation and the search for those unreached are conducted by church volunteers.

When Diane's crew of helpers did find Sopheap, she was lying in a hospital bed in her own waste. The Sunrise staff barely recognized the young woman who had withered away to a weight of 53 pounds. Sopheap was wrapped in a filthy, patched and matted shawl, and for upwards of two weeks had not yet been treated by a physician. She had no money to pay for medicines, no social status to leverage for her care. In Cambodia, hospitals typically expect the patients and their families, including the most indigent, to both purchase medications and provide basic care. Diane and her team had seen this kind of neglect in hospitals before, but Sopheap's case still came as a shock. Diane's staff pleaded with doctors to treat her or at least test her for TB, which often accompanies AIDS.

When it became apparent that the hospital staff was not going to care for Sopheap, the Sunrise staff and volunteers cleaned her, and over a period of several visits, ventured to ask that Sopheap be released into Sunrise's care. It is always a risk for a nonfamily member to ask Cambodian doctors for permission to take a patient out of their care. In seeking this permission, the implication, of course, is that the hospital staff members are not doing a good job, and consequently, they lose face. Diane's staff members asked and were repeatedly denied. So the Sunrise team returned regularly to clean Sopheap and to ask permission, again and again. Eventually, Diane went to the hospital in person, and with the kind of persistence of the widow in the parable in Luke 18:1-8, she won out. The doctors released Sopheap into Sunrise's care on a Friday, with a final, chilly comment: "Why do you want her? She has nothing. And she's just going to die anyway."

Sopheap wrapped an arm around Diane's neck in complete trust. Diane carried her to the one bathroom in the ward, a lavatory without a door. There Diane and the Sunrise helpers sponge-bathed Sopheap in the first full cleaning she had had in weeks, in front of the entire ward. It was an unusual sight, a vision of mercy in a place that desperately needed to see good news. The team dressed Sopheap in pretty, brightly colored clothes and took her to the Sunrise hospice.

Relieved to get out of the hospital, at first Sopheap seemed content to simply die peacefully. She let her food sit untasted. No one at Sunrise pushed her to eat, but Diane and her staff stroked her hair and her face; and because she was deaf, they connected with her without words. Diane indicated that eating meals was up to Sopheap, but she also communicated that Sopheap was of great value and that God loved her.

The next morning, Sopheap awoke, unafraid, in a place that was safe and secure and, consequently, she shook off the fatalism she had resigned herself to in the hospital. She ate breakfast, and afterward walked carefully with assistance outdoors and lay down in a hammock. One of the other Sunrise patients picked flowers for Sopheap and laid them in her pocket. Sopheap smiled and was at peace.

That Sunday morning, June 28, 2003, half a world away, President Bush made headlines when he declared that the war in Iraq was not over. Indeed, he confirmed that the war had accelerated and U.S. servicemen were increasingly subject to random violent attacks. The U.S. would need to commit troops long-term, the president clarified.

In the Middle East, Palestinian leaders urged small Palestinian factions beyond Hamas to join in the first complete suspension of violence in 33 months.

In Los Angeles, the Dodgers lost 3 to 1 to the California Angels and dropped three games behind San Francisco in the National League West.

In Paris, actress Ludivine Sagnier, a name meaning "divine light," was feted as the latest French cinematic export to America in a long line of actresses including Brigitte Bardot, Catherine Deneuve and Audrey Tautou.[54]

In Cambodia, there was nothing about Sopheap's sojourn with us in InnerCHANGE that would make the news. But it was, nevertheless, quietly remarkable to Diane and her team. Sopheap woke early after sleeping comfortably and, having tasted Sunrise's unusual quality of compassion, took the initiative to call for a bath. Afterward, she quickly grew tired, lay back contentedly and closed her eyes. Five minutes later she died peacefully.

I wonder how God receives the soul of a woman like Sopheap? Although Sopheap was unable to hear, Diane and her crew shared Christ with her through their actions, expressions, and their persistent pursuit of her as one of God's valuable children. Was it enough? I don't know. I do know this: God ordained that Sopheap's last three days with Sunrise were a divine appointment. And though her brief, brutal life and tragic passing did not garner headlines, did not even make a local obituary, I believe every moment of her last three days was front-page news in God's upside-down kingdom. Sopheap was the last patient to come in to fill Sunrise, and the first to pass on.

Three days. Three days is a long weekend for most of us. In three days, a professional consultant can deliver a concise and hard-hitting seminar. Three days can mean a luxury weekend for a prominent CEO. In that amount of time, a house painter can prep and prime a couple of rooms and get a single coat of paint down. In three days, a university student can research and write a 10-page paper under pressure. In three days, the Son of man delivered Himself up to be crucified, buried and rise again.

In three days, Diane Moss folded a broken woman into the welcoming arms of Sunrise and then released her gently into the waiting arms of Jesus.

I've rarely had occasion to tell Sopheap's story in the years since she died. I don't tell it here because it is one of our classic success stories. For success, I could tell any number of other stories about AIDS patients who have come to Sunrise, found relief and met Christ. In fact, quite a few who have come to Sunrise, who appeared to be dying, have responded well to love and care and recovered enough to rejoin their families.

I tell Sopheap's story here because she lived invisibly in the world's eyes. In fact, her last three days with us could be seen as a loose thread in a clumsily stitched pilgrimage. There was little glamour in Sopheap's life. Hurting people often come to us as she did, seemingly too far-gone, too late, with a pain they've backpacked so long that they don't remember what it is to stand upright. This story compels me with its stark reality. It reminds me that if we, the people of God, are going to meet the Sopheaps of this world squarely, as Christ did, we are going to have to reach into the deepest pockets of our souls and pull out more than the loose change of the world's clichés.

Missions Sunday

A couple of years ago, a good friend sent me a sermon on tape from an affluent "mega-church." The sermon was from Missions Sunday at the church, and a faint hope stirred within me that this would be a sermon that would catalyze new efforts for the Kingdom. The pastor took his text from Ecclesiastes, and I found myself increasingly drawn in as he shared about need and suffering in the world. Cautiously, he began to poke and prod at the congregation, suggesting that a Southern California lifestyle was not at all reflective of standards of living the world over.

"Uncertainty and risk are the norm," he stated emphatically, "because it is in our desperation that God wants to meet us." I held my breath as he drove toward the climax. Could it be that this pastor was actually going to call for simpler living, sacrificial giving or greater participation in world mission?

"So what am I saying? That you should sell all and move to South Africa or Afghanistan?"

"Yes," I breathed.

"I wish it were that easy," he said with a sigh. I could picture him shaking his head sensibly. After all, the people in this congregation were movers and shakers in their industries, embedded in the "real world." Many had invested heavily in their educations and logged long hours in the workplace to shoulder their way into the ranks of "successful" people in a very competitive market. At last, the pastor admitted that he was not suggesting that everyone sell all and head to the field. My attention waned with my disappointment. He proceeded with some "clever" comments about missionary attire, the "dated fashions and 1970s haircuts." There was an approving murmur from the audience, now comfortably off the hook. He closed with a story about a blind skier as exhortation that we must step out in faith. The message was clear. It was up to the individual to determine how he or she should step out *in their current environment*. And some would go home, believing they had been fed by the message, when perhaps, instead, they were hooked up, IV-fashion, to a church service that didn't disturb, didn't demand.

"I wish it were that easy." Upon reflection, I was more than disappointed—I was mad. I thought about the good people I know in the field, planting churches in difficult places in Asia and doing community development in Africa. I thought, also, about their decisions to temper cultural individualism and work for transformation among the poor in mission community with others. There are lots of appropriate words to describe their sacrificial relocations to such places—and their willingness to stay on. "Easy" is not one of them.

Pouring Our Oil on the Feet of the City

When I see with my mind's eye the vivid picture of Diane and her team gently bathing Sopheap in the doorless toilet; when I recall the scent of fresh towels and clean, folded clothes, I remember another woman 2,000 years before, bathing the feet of Jesus with her tears and a precious oil. Both women engaged in expressions of love that were unorthodox, perhaps flirting with the edges of propriety. Both actions could be seen as costly expenditures for marginal utility, yet both are eminently memorable. Finally, both actions represented anointments for burial.

In our work, we always find voices raised to suggest that we could be making more efficient, effective use of our lives elsewhere—and logic seems to be on their side. Consider John's account of Mary's anointing of Jesus:

> Six days before the Passover Jesus came to Bethany, the home of Lazarus, whom he had raised from the dead. There they gave a dinner for him. Martha served, and Lazarus was one of those at the table with him. Mary took a pound of costly perfume made of pure nard,

anointed Jesus' feet, and wiped them with her hair. The house was filled with the fragrance of the perfume. But Judas Iscariot, one of his disciples (the one who was about to betray him), said, "Why was this perfume not sold for three hundred denarii and the money given to the poor?" (He said this not because he cared about the poor, but because he was a thief; he kept the common purse and used to steal what was put into it.) Jesus said, "Leave her alone. She bought it so that she might keep it for the day of my burial. You always have the poor with you, but you do not always have me" (John 12:1-8).

Forget for a moment that this was Judas and that he was wrong in the heart from the start. Isn't there some merit to his complaint that Mary's valuable perfume should have been sold on behalf of the poor instead of slopped over Jesus' feet? At the very least, if Mary was determined to squander her perfume, shouldn't it at least have been used in the conventional way, to anoint Jesus' head? Instead, she poured it all over His feet, the humblest part of the body, and on to the floor. Logic seemed to be on Judas's side that day. Mary's precious perfume could have been used to outfit many ministries among the poor for any number of days.

At InnerCHANGE, our members are our most valuable assets. Many were educated at the highest levels society can offer, in the most distinguished schools. Others have come off the street and bring with them their unique vision and inimitable skills and experiences. All of our members are tremendously talented and energetic. Each one could be making an impact in a more "prestigious" field. Yet our members continue to pour out their precious lives all over the humblest parts of the globe. Our members spend their lives in areas of society that, like the feet, get the most wear and tear, perform the most menial jobs and receive the least glory.

Paul Smith pours out his Harvard-educated life for young men in Los Angeles. Jenny Bacon, a Guatemalan with unique entrepreneurial skills and extraordinary passion and energy, immigrated to the U.S. and could easily have created her own version of the American Dream. Instead, she and husband, Nate, a Stanford graduate, seek out gang-bangers on the streets of the Mission District and in San Francisco's Juvenile Hall. I think of John Tiersma Watson, talented poet and artist. He could be making his mark in the art world but has taken his gift of uncommon insight to the marginalized and has empowered former taggers and street youth to form an artists' cooperative called L.A. Street Productions. Then there is Tammy Fong Heilemann, a Berkeley graduate who spent more than five years rescuing girls sold into prostitution in Kampong Cham, Cambodia.

Perhaps, in the world's eyes, we could be making more appropriate use of our lives elsewhere. Think of all that skill and energy, like Mary's perfume, poured out on the feet of the city. To Judas, such an act was a waste, a mess. Judas is, in some ways, an apostle of the pharisaism of the twenty-first century. Today we find that some of the smugness of the Pharisees is perhaps less *religious* than it is *professional*—a favorite expression used today to ground idealism being, "In the real world . . ." or "In the corporate world . . ." Certainly, with that perspective today, many would line up with Judas and declare Mary's act a waste.

But it was, in fact, a thing of beauty. In Mark's version of this story, Jesus made clear that Mary's act was a good deed, using the Greek word for "good" that also translates as "beautiful." Jesus claimed it was such an important act that the world would never forget it.

Mary's anointing was also a meaningful act. Like the account of Mary, many of the members of our communities spill out their lives in areas doomed to die. No matter what we do toward transformation in every community we choose to live in, some will not make it. Some will be bulldozed, sold out, gentrified or redeveloped for a "better" crowd. And our hopes and dreams, joined with those of the poor, will simply be an expenditure of love, an anointing for burial. Logic may be on Judas's side. But for those who choose to pour out their lives among the poor, there will be a fragrance that fills the house of God.

afterword

Having observed InnerCHANGE primarily through the life and lens of John Hayes, whom I have known up close and personal in recent years, I see a modern chapter in the age-old struggle of Jesus' followers balancing community and mission.

At a fundamental theological level, I see the passion of John Hayes and his colleagues as an attempt to integrate both the whole of the Trinity and the whole of both Old and New Testaments in the context of world mission in the modern urban world. And in this they follow a rich tradition.

For a generation, New Testament scholar Robert Banks and other scholars have been teaching us that the earliest Christian impulses were to gather together in house groups that integrated generations, to hold classes centered on Scripture study, and to share Eucharistic meals that led them into the world on mission.

Early Church scholar Dervas Chitty reminds us that large numbers of Christians formed desert cities in what Perry Miller used to call the Church's "errand into the wilderness," and these prophetic communities were born to balance the encrusted pastoral communities of Christians.

Another scholar, named Herbert B. Workman, coined the phrase "the evolution of the monastic ideal" by reminding us that while the first monks were *mono* and alone in deserts, almost immediately community monasticism was born with Anthony and flourished in the disintegrating Western European middle ages as a result of following the spirituality of Benedict of Nursia, who published his "Rule" for how communities of lay monks should live, work, worship and serve in mission after A.D. 529. Some 300 Benedictine communities, all without outside funding, and located in many of the toughest places, integrated work, worship and discipline, transformed communities and created the foundations of modern Europe.

Francis and Dominic emerged from different paths to remind us again of the two sides of discipleship reflected in the Great Commandment. For Dominic, theology was essentially loving God with the mind, while for Francis it was faith active in love. Dominic built faculties of theology to probe the mysteries of God, and within a generation gave us Thomas Aquinas. Francis took the gospel to the streets to find, live with and serve the poor. These are two sides of the discipleship coin, of course, but fraught with tension. They are corrective of the extremes of each other. As a community, InnnerCHANGE seeks to balance these two approaches.

From the Protestant Reformation to the present, we have witnessed what Donald Dayton calls the "three tributaries of modern evangelism." The sixteenth-century Lutherans, the eighteenth-century Wesleyans and, finally, the nineteenth-century traditions emerging from other awakenings (holiness, dispensationalist and fundamentalist tributaries)—each has incubated forms of community. It took 30 years of war in Germany to shape Spener, Francke and Zinzendorf into a communitarian spirituality that sought to reform German Lutheranism from the bottom up, and clearly influenced Wesley's journey and the Methodist movements that followed. Continental Calvinism and English Puritanism have some nuanced differences, but both spun out communitarian impulses.

I had the privilege of living and serving Christ for 35 years in one of the 77 neighborhoods of inner-city Chicago. The Jesus People community lived and served in the contiguous neighborhood of Uptown. Good News North of Howard community resided in the Jonquil Hotel on the Evanston border; and several neighborhoods west of me, I watched the famous Circle Church morph into the Circle Community. There were other Anabaptist-influenced communities in the area as well; and in the Catholic community, I became great friends with the Shalom Community.

All of these communities emerged, sharing and living common spiritual life in the very bastions of Evangelicalism symbolized by another Trinity that included Moody, Trinity and Wheaton. I learned early on in Chicago that in a disintegrating urban world, mainline churches and their institutions, be they Catholic, Protestant, Evangelical or Charismatic, serve as spiritual supermarkets that survive best in homogeneous cultures, like American suburbs. But in port-of-entry communities, or among the most marginalized of diverse peoples, these communities reinvent church for growing numbers. And among the more elite cultures and classes, I have witnessed a shift in culture from the need for power to the need for intimacy. Hence the growing need for ministries like InnerCHANGE.

Thanks to some Latin American scholars, we talk a lot about action/reflection models of learning in this generation. I first met InnerCHANGE when this community was in its action phase. In the past couple of years, the leaders have relocated from San Francisco and elsewhere to reflect on God's action in the world, and what they were learning as a community. Now, after some agonizing struggles that I've heard about only briefly, they are relocating to London and re-engaging for global mission. This new book distills what they have learned on their incredible journey, which I so admire. I close my little essay with a benediction:

To God be the glory, and to the earth be peace;
To InnerCHANGE be courage, and to the world be hope.

Ray Bakke
Chairman, Board of Regents
Bakke Graduate University of Ministry

endnotes

1. Jean Luc Krieg, "Slum Sector Report," published by Geneva Global Inc., July 2004, pp. 1-2.
2. "Missions Today by the Numbers," *Brigada Today* newsletter, April 14, 2006. This brief article summarizes research done by Bill and Amy Stearns who have concluded that the number of U.S. missionaries sent out has declined 46 percent since 1988 when 65,000 were on the field. The number in 2006 is closer to 35,000.
3. Jimmy Carter, "Challenges for Humanity, A Beginning," *National Geographic*, February 2002, pp. 2-3. For information on advertising expenditures, see Crain Communications, "2006 Fact Pack; Fourth Annual Guide to Advertising and Marketing," 2006.
4. Ibid. For greater detail on the gap between rich and poor countries, see Jeffrey D. Sachs, *The End of Poverty, Economic Possibilities of Our Time*, (London: Penguin Books Ltd., 2004), pp. 29-31.
5. "Tighter Intellectual Property Rights," *Straits Times*, October 26, 1999, Singapore, p. 37.
6. Peronet Despeignes, "Census: Poverty Rose by 1M in '03," *USA Today*, (Fri/Sat/Sun, Aug. 27-29, 2004), p.
7. Ibid. For greater detail on the gap between rich and poor countries, see Jeffrey D. Sachs, *The End of Poverty, Economic Possibilities of Our Time* (London: Penguin Books Ltd., 2004), pp. 29-31. Also, consult the current World Bank Atlas.
8. Robert Wuthnow, *The Crisis in the Churches: Spiritual Malaise, Fiscal Woe* (New York: Oxford University Press, 1997), p. 141.
9. John L. Ronsvalle and Sylvia Ronsvalle, *The State of Church Giving Through 2000* (Champaign, IL: Empty Tomb, 2002), p. 40. Despite growing wealth in North America, church members gave proportionally more during the Great Depression (3.3 percent of income) than church members do now.
10. World Bank Atlas 1999, p. 16.
11. Sachs, *The End of Poverty, Economic Possibilities of Our Time*, p. 51.
12. James A. Inciardi and Hilary L. Surratt, "Children in the Streets of Brazil: Drug Use, Crime, Violence, and HIV Risks," Substance Use and Misuse, 1997, p. 1.
13. U. S. Dept. of State, "Trafficking in Persons Report," June 5, 2002, released by The Office to Monitor and Combat Trafficking in Persons.
14. Patricia Wittberg, *The Rise and Fall of Catholic Religious Orders, a Social Movement Perspective* (New York: State University of New York Press, 1994), pp. 213-214.
15. Not surprisingly, St. Francis's life has encouraged many biographies. He was a historical figure of enormous significance. My short compilation of the critical events of St. Francis's life, particularly his break with his father, is drawn largely from three sources: Johannes Jorgensen, *St. Francis of Assisi* (New York: Image Books, 1955), pp. 40-58; G. K. Chesterton, *St. Francis of Assisi* (New York: Image Books, 1987), n.p.; C. H. Lawrence, *The Friars* (London: Longman Group UK Ltd., 1994), pp. 26-42.
16. Ibid.
17. Ibid.
18. Lawrence, *The Friars*, pp. 166-180.
19. Ibid., see especially pp. 202-228.

20. John Wesley, *Journals* (entry for May 21, 1764). John Wesley's journals are now variously available. See, for example, Reginald Ward and Richard Hietzenrater, ed., *The Works of John Wesley, Journals and Diaries V* (Nashville, TN; Abingdon Press, 1993).
21. Ronald Rolheiser, *The Holy Longing* (New York: Doubleday, 1999), p. 64.
22. Lawrence, *The Friars*, pp. 1-25.
23. Michel Mollat, *The Poor in the Middle Ages* (New Haven, CT: Yale University Press, 1986), p. 123.
24. G. K. Chesterton, *St. Francis of Assisi* (New York: Image Books, 1987), foreword.
25. Lawrence, pp. 15-19.
26. Anthony J. Gittins, "Affonso," from *Biographical Dictionary of Christian Mission*. ed. Gerald H. Anderson (Grand Rapids, MI: Eerdmans, 1998), p. 6. See also, Stephen Neill, *A History of Christian Missions*, 2 ed. (Middlesex, England: Viking Penguin Inc., 1986), p. 118.
27. Scott Bessenecker, *The New Friars*, p. 3. At the time of this writing, Scott's book is currently in manuscript form, soon to be released by InterVarsity Press.
28. Bono, in Sachs, *The End of Poverty, Economic Possibilities for Our Time*, p. xv.
29. "Damien of Molokai," from *Biographical Dictionary of Christian Missions*, ed. Gerald H. Anderson (Grand Rapids, MI: Eerdmans, 1998), p. 167.
30. Mollat, *The Poor in the Middle Ages*, p. 23. The phrase "to follow naked the naked Christ" originated with St. Jerome, an Early Church father.
31. Chesterton, *St. Francis of Assisi*, p. 101.
32. Unpublished author discussion with Bob Ekblad at the InnerCHANGE conference, June 2005.
33. Stephen Neill, *A History of Christian Missions*, 2nd ed. (New York: Viking Penguin, 1986), p. 40.
34. Ibid., pp. 37-38.
35. John Piper, *A Hunger for God* (Wheaton, IL: Crossway, 1997). John Piper has an excellent chapter on Isaiah 58 in this book called "Finding God in the Garden of Pain," pp. 125-153.
36. Stuart Murray, *Church After Christendom* (Milton Keynes, UK: Paternoster Press, 2004), pp. 136-137.
37. Dr. Bobby Clinton, from remarks made in a Fuller Seminary Class, June 1994.
38. *Merriam-Webster's Collegiate Dictionary*, 10th ed. (Springfield, MA: Merriam-Webster, Inc., 2002), p. 816.
39. One of the best short histories of the expansion of the friars, particularly the Franciscans and Dominicans, can be found in C. H. Lawrence, *The Friars* (London: Longman Group UK, Ltd., 1994), especially chapter 11, "Afar Unto the Gentiles," pp. 203-221.
40. Unpublished author discussion with Evan Howard, director of Spirituality Shoppe, August 6, 2002.
41. Unpublished author telephone conversation with Rob Yackley, founder of Nieu Communities, May 2, 2006.
42. Gerald Arbuckle, *Out of Chaos: Refounding Religious Congregations* (London: Cassell Publishers, 1988), p. 44.
43. Pol Pot led a communist rebellion and was prime minister of Cambodia (Democratic Kampuchea) from 1976 to 1979. Under his rule, large numbers of people were held in camps or forcibly relocated to the countryside, and an estimated three million

people died. His reign of terror is documented in the book and movie *The Killing Fields*. Those Cambodians who lost their lives are remembered at a national genocide memorial just outside Phnom Penh.

44. Belden Lane, *The Solace of Fierce Landscapes* (Oxford: Oxford Press, 1998), p 152.
45. Mollat, *The Poor in the Middle Ages*, p. 10.
46. Ibid., pp. 38-41.
47. Kenneth Scott Latourette, *A History of Christianity* (Peabody, MA: Prince Press, 1997), pp. 342-347. See also George G. Hunter III, *The Celtic Way of Evangelism* (Nashville, TN: Abingdon Press, 2000), pp. 26-40.
48. Neill, *A History of Christian Mission*, pp. 60-61.
49. Simon Schama, *A History of Britain* (London: BBC Worldwide Ltd., 2000), pp. 53-60.
50. Lee Palmer Wandel, *Always Among Us, Images of the Poor in Zwingli's Zurich* (Cambridge, UK: Cambridge University Press, 1990), p. 61.
51. Ibid., p. 176
52. Lawrence, *The Friars*, pp. 29-34.
53. Ibid., pp. 60-64.
54. The article on President Bush and his pronouncements on the Iraq War as well as the standing of the Dodgers came from *Los Angeles Times*, June 28, 2003. The glimpse into Palestinian factions in the Middle East came from James Bennett, "The Mideast Gaining Ground," *New York Times*, June 28, 2003, Section 4, p. 2. Finally, the article on Ludivine Sagnier came from Marshall Heyman, "Ludivine Sagnier; City of Light's Bright Star," *New York Times*, June 29, 2003, Section 9, p. 4.

thanks

"It takes a community to reach a community" is a saying we coined in InnerCHANGE to capture the essence of our collective impact as missionaries among the poor. I have found in writing *sub-merge* that it has taken a community to produce this book. In many ways, I feel that I have compiled the book more than written it, creating a mosaic from the stories and insights of our members and friends in other mission entities serving among the poor.

First and foremost, I thank my wife and two daughters for their constant support over the several years that *sub-merge* has been in process. There *is* no book without my family. Second, I thank my InnerCHANGE family for their unflagging belief in this effort as well as their commitment to contribute stories and ideas, and to read over the manuscript. I am particularly indebted to Tim Lockie and Darren Prince, who made significant sacrifices of time to read over and help me rework critical chapters of this book. I'd also like to thank our neighbors in the poor communities in which we have sub-merged. Without their belief in us as people, and their priceless friendship, *sub-merge* could not have been written.

Beyond InnerCHANGE and our communities among the poor, it is hard for me to imagine *sub-merge* without the addition of critical ideas from my artist-in-ministry in Melbourne, Nick Wight. Indeed, the very name "sub-merge" was Nick's idea, and he worked countless hours with me to help lay out our work with artistic power. Hillary Prag, Zoe Mullery and Tom Wells are friends who lent reading time to *sub-merge*. All three gave me valuable feedback. I must especially thank Ray Bakke and John

Perkins for the inspiration they have been to me and for their personal encouragement through the years. In a time when Christian leaders often struggle to responsibly follow after the apostle Paul's dictum, "Imitate me as I imitate Christ," I have found these two men exceptionally willing to model an upside-down faith in urban settings in a way that is both humble and compelling. Tom Sine, Judy Lingenfelter, Evan Howard, Jon Sharpe, Alan Hirsch, Scottie May and Mick Duncan have also all been amazingly willing to extend themselves personally to help nudge InnerCHANGE along, and consequently helped in the formation of *sub-merge*. I am indebted to Viv Grigg, friend, and author of *Companion to the Poor*, for his fearless call for incarnational orders among the poor and his unflinching dedication to empowering workers from among the poor worldwide. I cannot begin to sum up the debt we owe many other women and men whose writing stimulated and liberated us to pursue callings among the poor.

Finally, I thank Ash and Anji Barker of Urban Neighbors of Hope. Their special friendship over the years for me, personally, as well as for InnerCHANGE, has been of incalculable impact as we have woven together as companion orders among the poor in a sharpening way.

about CRM and InnerCHANGE

CRM (Church Resource Ministries) is a movement committed to developing leaders to strengthen and multiply the Church worldwide.

Over 300 CRM missionaries live and minister in nations on every continent, coaching, mentoring and apprenticing those called to lead and serve the Christian movement in their settings. This results in the multiplication of godly leaders who have a passion for their world and who are empowered to multiply their lives and ministry. Through them, CRM stimulates movements of fresh, authentic churches, holistic in nature, so that the name of God is renowned among the nations.

InnerCHANGE is a Christian order among the poor within CRM. InnerCHANGE is composed of communities of missionaries living and ministering incarnationally among the most marginalized, striving to follow the Lord God's injunction "to do justice, love mercy, and to walk humbly with our God" (Mic. 6:8).

InnerCHANGE missionaries live in neighborhoods of poverty around the world as church planters, community organizers and church developers, but most important, as neighbors. InnerCHANGE staff pursue a style of community life befitting an order, placing the well-being of people and the quality of their relationships before programs and purposefully providing for the lifelong personal development of those called to share themselves with the needy.

More information about CRM and specifically about InnerCHANGE—locations, values, short-term experiences, internships and longer apprenticeships—can be found at:

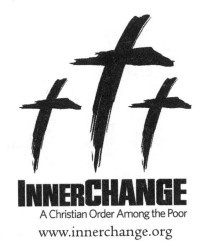

InnerCHANGE
A Christian Order Among the Poor
www.innerchange.org

CRM EMPOWERING LEADERS
www.crmleaders.org

Read more about submerging and
John Hayes's blog at
http://submergebook.com/